SOUNDBITE

SOUNDBITE

THE ADMISSIONS SECRET
THAT GETS YOU
INTO COLLEGE AND BEYOND

SARA HARBERSON

Go
hachette
BOOKS
NEW YORK

Hachette Go, an imprint of Hachette Books
Hachette Book Group
1290 Avenue of the Americas
New York, NY 10104
HachetteGo.com
Facebook.com/HachetteGo
Instagram.com/HachetteGo

First Edition: April 2021

Hachette Books is a division of Hachette Book Group, Inc.

The Hachette Go and Hachette Books name and logos are trademarks of Hachette Book Group, Inc.

The publisher is not responsible for websites (or their content) that are not owned by the publisher.

Print book interior design by Trish Wilkinson.

Library of Congress Cataloging-in-Publication Data

Names: Harberson, Sara, author.
Title: Soundbite: the admissions secret that gets you into college and beyond / by Sara Harberson.
Description: New York: Hachette Go, [2021]
Identifiers: LCCN 2020047867 | ISBN 9780306874833 (paperback) | ISBN 9780306874826 (ebook)
Subjects: LCSH: Universities and colleges—Admission—United States. | College choice—United States.
Classification: LCC LB2351.2 .H35 2021 | DDC 378.1/610973—dc23
LC record available at https://lccn.loc.gov/2020047867

ISBNs: 978-0-306-87483-3 (trade paperback); 978-0-306-87482-6 (ebook)

Printed in the United States of America

LSC-C

Printing 2, 2022

Contents

Author's Note — ix

Introduction — xi

PART 1 UNDERSTANDING THE SOUNDBITE

CHAPTER 1 Four Years Reduced to Four Minutes — 3

CHAPTER 2 Find Your Defining Statement — 9

CHAPTER 3 The Power of the Soundbite — 19

CHAPTER 4 Evolution of the Soundbite — 25

CHAPTER 5 Be Honest About Your Strengths and Limitations (Self-Awareness) — 43

CHAPTER 6 Avoid Following the Crowd (Intentionality) — 57

CHAPTER 7 Be Willing to Tell Your Story (Storytelling) — 97

CHAPTER 8 A Time and Place for Soundbite — 123

PART 2 CRAFTING YOUR SOUNDBITE

CHAPTER 9 Get to Work on #lifegoals 133

CHAPTER 10 The Soundbite Rules 145

PART 3 LIVING YOUR SOUNDBITE

CHAPTER 11 The College List 189

CHAPTER 12 The Homegrown Idea 215

CHAPTER 13 The Special-Special 227

CHAPTER 14 The Pivot 235

CHAPTER 15 Decisions 241

CHAPTER 16 Soundbite Now and for the Future 249

Conclusion 253

*Appendix A: Helpful Exercises When You Have Trouble
   Coming Up with Your Soundbite* 257

Appendix B: Examples of Soundbites That Worked 263

Appendix C: Extra Soundbites and Essay Topics 271

Acknowledgments 281

Author's Note

This book includes examples of real students I have worked with and those I continue to work with. Actual leadership positions, activities, colleges, and other identifiable traits were replaced with other details of equal relevance and status to ensure confidentiality. I wanted to retain the power of my students' stories and Soundbites without compromising their identities.

Introduction

People often ask me how I got the name "America's College Counselor." It sounds quite official, like someone anointed me with it, like a world leader or journalist. The truth is that I gave it to myself. Pretty bold, right? Yes, indeed.

No one can say it is not true. No one can say I cannot use it. I have simply taken three words from the English language and put them together. And no combination could be more accurate about me than those three words. I have the degrees, experience, and titles to prove it.

But what makes it so authentic for me is that there is not a day or hour that goes by when I am not actively being America's College Counselor. Sure, I have private clients and an active subscription-based program, Application Nation, for families with college-bound children. But most of what I offer is free to everyone: monthly Facebook Live sessions, online guides, videos, a weekly blog, and weekly Instagram Lives for anyone who wants to follow me. *I am the college counselor for all.*

It is who I am, how I define myself, and how others see me. In fact, it is how I introduce myself in my Facebook Live and Instagram Live sessions. It is now part of my professional branding:

I am America's College Counselor.

This sentence is my Soundbite. My identity. My daily motivation. My mantra. And I won't make any apologies for it because it is my truth. No one had to give it to me. I gave it to myself, and I work hard every day to live it.

As Americans, we focus on educational degrees, job titles, and leadership positions that others grant us, confer upon us, or elect us to. We wait for these milestones to happen in our lives. Finishing four years of college. Getting that promotion. Finally being recognized by peers that we are the top dog.

Why wait for others to give us something? Why wait for others to give us permission to make a positive impact?

No matter what initials precede or follow our names, they are simply a formality. Just because someone has an impressive degree or title doesn't mean they are using it to live a fulfilling life—one that contributes to the greater good.

Consider the high school student who gets elected as president of student government by his peers. This might be the most coveted, traditional leadership role a college applicant could have on his application. Yet admissions officers (called AOs by insiders) would never know if the student leaned on his cabinet members to do all the work. The admissions officers would care only about that title, right? Wrong.

What happens if you are the person who makes the real contribution to student government or to the school? Would you let others take the credit or take charge? As long as it is the truth, the student who does the bulk of the work can list the tremendous impact she has made on her own application's activities list. I want her to recognize that it is about not only what she does but how she presents that in her application and to others. She could also make sure her college counselor and teachers writing letters of recommendation on her behalf know the *real story* as well.

What about the individual who gets into a highly regarded college because of money and lies? Or the person who ends up relying on family and connections to get professional opportunities instead of earning her way? It can seem so unfair to all of us "regular folks."

Some say that is the way the world works. I say that is how the world works for a small fraction of the population. The rest of us need to navigate every step of our lives using our own ingenuity to achieve our goals. However, the process can seem so overwhelming and the prize of acceptance out of reach at times for regular folks like you and me.

Soundbite gives all of us not only hope but a real action plan to live our lives and achieve goals we have for our future. Once we identify the skills, traits, and experiences of our life that no one else could put together in exactly the same way, we have the beginnings of a Soundbite for ourselves. As long as we have the proof to back up our Soundbite because we are living it every day, we can be our own best advocate. It is the most empowering thing we can do for ourselves, no matter our age or individual goals.

The wondrous piece of the Soundbite is that it can be embraced at whatever stage of the process you are in. Whether the student is a high school freshman or a high school senior, *Soundbite* can help. In fact, adults who want to attend college, change careers, or pursue a fresh start can benefit from this approach. It is never too soon or too late to write, embrace, and live your Soundbite. I often say that I wish I had recognized and celebrated who I was much earlier in life. Now, I don't waste a day trying to be anything but my best self, my Soundbite.

By picking up this book and getting started, you are taking charge of a process that most people believe leaves little room for students to dictate their outcomes. Yet the more empowered students are, the more control they actually have. The key is understanding how to use the power effectively to determine your future. This book is for parents, students, college counselors, teachers, and anyone who values opportunity for themselves and the most deserving young people.

As I mentioned, I am the college counselor for all. I don't just help students who want to attend certain colleges; I help students who want to attend college.

Ivy League universities may have cachet in certain communities, but college is college. Students can get an incredible education at almost any college in the country. It is never about where you go; it is about what you do with the opportunity. And the same philosophy applies to high school as well. It is never the school that defines you; it is what you do while you are there.

If we understand ourselves so well, we will recognize which environments are better for us in a given moment. For those who value an Ivy League university but feel it is out of reach, that doesn't mean it is out of the realm of possibility. It might just mean you will get there, down the road. Like me.

I attended a small, relatively unknown liberal arts college back in the day. It set the stage for everything in this book. I later worked at an Ivy League university and got my graduate degree from there. But it was college that transformed me because it ended up being the right place for me at the right time. Understanding where we thrive best in the moment is just as important as understanding ourselves.

College changes lives. College changes one's trajectory.

But over the last several decades, families have lost faith in the college admissions process. They have watched good kids get squeezed out or disadvantaged. Times are changing though. The Varsity Blues admissions scandal of 2019 and the COVID-19 pandemic of 2020 shifted the balance. Long gone are the days when colleges can get away with unfair practices.

The landscape is still as competitive as ever; yet we are ushering in a new era in which a good kid instead of a less deserving kid becomes the poster child for a college education.

To anyone who says we need money, connections, and others to get what we want, I say, "Not true." All I need is my Soundbite, and I can be the person I want to be. So can you.

PART 1

UNDERSTANDING THE

SOUNDBITE

CHAPTER 1

Four Years Reduced to Four Minutes

When I first started working in the field as an admissions officer at the University of Pennsylvania, I was expected to read twenty-five applications a day. The applicant pool numbers were at an all-time high at Penn, but I still felt like I could get to know some of the students applying, especially in the Early Decision round. Each application was *supposed* to take twenty minutes or so to read. But on average, a review took me between twenty-five and thirty minutes—and many times a lot longer. If I got behind on a particular day, which often happened, I could catch up at night and on the weekends, as we were permitted at that time to work from home during the reading season. As much as I loved this part of the process, it was grueling. Outside a few breaks each day, there was enormous pressure to get through thousands of applications in a short amount of time.

Even though I became a "speed reader" (as most AOs do), each application took time as I was required to take notes on each section and formulate a clear final statement explaining why I was recommending a specific admissions decision. For example, if I recommended an acceptance or a denial after reading the application, I had to articulate a very good reason for it in one sentence:

> The SAT score is a bit low for a premed applicant in our pool, but his straight-A record with AP Calculus and AP Biology suggests he can handle the premed curriculum, and his responsibility of taking care of his elderly grandparent allows me to see him working with dementia patients one day in the future—ADMIT.

Or this:

> Really strong test scores across the board with straight As too, but the student doesn't distinguish himself in the sea of premed applicants—DENY.

It took a lot of practice to be able to take an entire application and distill it down into one sentence. Some of my sentences were longer than others; some were less complimentary too. Knowing the competition at Penn, yet not necessarily knowing the applicant firsthand most of the time, made it easier to be more objective and unemotional when it came to summing up the student. It came down to a one-sentence summary. At Penn, we called that sentence a "bottom line," a name that seemed to evoke a sense of toughness. The reality was there was no sugarcoating going on at Penn unless the student really impressed an admissions officer.

Truthfully, for some of us, we were the opposite of unemotional. I was too invested at times. But Penn's decisive approach forced all of us to remove any emotion from our evaluation and simply get to the "bottom line." There was no time to get behind a student who did not have a shot, and the term "bottom line" was representative of Penn's admissions process. But there are many different terms used by admissions offices to describe the same thing: "final thought," "last word," or simply "recommendation."

My term, "Soundbite," is another name for what every AO has to do after reading an application. It acknowledges the swiftness of this process, yet reminds all of us to give people something they will remember.

All admissions officers at elite colleges are trained to write an overarching statement about each student. After the initial read of an application, the admissions officer doesn't have time to reread it fully every time the application is discussed. This statement comes in handy. It is also used as a crutch for those members of the admissions committee who don't read the application before voting on whether or not to admit the student. Yes, that's true. Most people weighing in on the decision do not read the application at all or in its entirety. They rely on that Soundbite (or whatever the admissions office calls it) written by the AO.

But Soundbite has dual meaning. While AOs come up with a Soundbite on each student, students should not sit back and hope for the best. They can and should write their own Soundbites—**not to be listed anywhere in the application but to inspire, transform, and determine how they see themselves and how AOs see them**.

And if their application is the embodiment of their Soundbite, the student is not only writing their own Soundbite but dramatically helping the AO write a more accurate version for them.

Given how quickly AOs will be reading an application and formulating a Soundbite, the student needs to take matters into their own hands. If the student has such a clear Soundbite and allows that one sentence to guide them through high school and the college admissions process, it will come through naturally in every section of their application—without them ever having to write it anywhere in the application.

That's the power of a Soundbite. It can literally transform how the student sees him- or herself and how the AO sees the student as well. Essentially, the student can make sure that the AO hits the nail on the head and writes a Soundbite that accurately reflects their own. It is essential to do this because AOs read through applications so quickly that if a student's identity and distinctiveness does not come through loud and clear, the AO's Soundbite on them will be decisive:

> This student did not stand out in our applicant pool—DENY.

If the reading process is rushed, the decision-making process for colleges feels like moving at warp speed. When I worked at Penn, a revolving door of five to ten AOs would be asked to present often two hundred plus applications each during a day of committee sessions. Committee was where we made final admissions decisions. Because we were making thousands of decisions a day, AOs relied on their "bottom line" (or Soundbite) to guide the discussion on each applicant. We only had a few *seconds* to read our bottom line and recommend an admissions decision.

Here's common dialogue between an AO and their supervisor during a committee session:

Supervisor: "Tell us about Jane Smith."

AO: "Jane Smith has one of the highest GPAs in the twenty applications we've received from her high school, but if you look closely, her curriculum is not nearly as strong as it could be—I recommend a denial."

Supervisor: "Denied it is. Next student."

Sometimes the chair of the committee would ask me questions. But most of the time, a decision was made instantaneously based on the bottom line I had written. When I became an associate dean at Penn and I was signing off on final decisions in committee, I relied on an AO's bottom line because I simply didn't have the time to go through each application as carefully as I wanted. Good or bad, the AO's one-sentence summary of each student guided every decision. The AO has more power in this process than one might think!

Knowing this, students have power too. It is time for students to reclaim that power and determine their futures. Soundbite is the answer.

Fast-forward to today: The admissions process at all elite colleges has become even more fast paced. Admissions officers are still being asked to write a final statement about each application they read, but time is of the essence. Penn recently acknowledged that all applications are being read and "decisioned" in the office during the regular workday. Long gone are the days when the AO had time to ponder and carefully review the application in the comfort of their own home. Penn also admits that their AOs must now read one hundred applications a day and spend only *four minutes per application*. This is a result of Penn's applicant pool growth: it is twice as large as it was twenty years ago.

Some elite colleges are experiencing even larger growth in their applicant pools. Yet few offices have increased their admissions staff to accommodate this exponential growth. These colleges have been forced to streamline the reading and selection process even more than Penn. If the students don't stand out beyond typically strong transcripts and test scores, they may not have a chance of admission.

But it is not just certain colleges whose admit rates are on the decline. Colleges that were once considered "backup" schools are now just as selective as an Ivy League university due to long-term recruitment strategies to get more applicants. Colleges can spend years cultivating a student to apply, only to spend minutes reading their application and seconds deciding their fate. If you are wondering why colleges will waive application fees, offer open houses, or overload your mailbox with glossy brochures, it is not because they want to admit you; they simply want you to apply. As colleges continue to refine institutional priorities, students feel like they are at the mercy of AOs.

Yet students have the power to change how they are viewed and take control of the process—*their* process. Soundbite will not only change the way they see themselves but how others see them.

CHAPTER 2

Find Your Defining Statement

The biggest concern I hear from students who are going through the college admissions process is that they don't want to be misunderstood. The shy student worries that admissions officers will misinterpret her reticence and peg her as disengaged. The ambitious student who takes the SAT five times to get the best score wonders if AOs will think he is overly concerned with test scores instead of his high school community. The student who is a member of a bunch of clubs, but not a leader, believes she will be viewed as a secondary contributor rather than a trailblazer. And the student who finally finds his passion during senior year or the student who is still searching for it wonders if he will be judged as not "college worthy."

Students' worries are valid. AOs are shockingly quick to judge. In actuality, we are all quick to judge. We begin to make assumptions based on where someone is from, what they are wearing, and how others have described them to us. Sometimes those assumptions are not even close to the reality of who that person is.

Back when I first started as an AO, the college application offered the option of including a photograph. The joke in the Penn Admissions Office was that if you wanted to admit a student, just swap the real picture of the student with a picture of a pretty girl (regardless of whether the real student identified as female or male), and our dean of admissions would admit the student on the spot. He went straight to the picture and made a decision. This was hardly a joke to me. I remember wondering, if this was done openly, what was happening when I was not looking.

The vast majority of colleges no longer ask for a picture in the application. But this memory is a sobering reminder that what a student puts forth in the admissions process (including the world of social media) and how they do it forms the AO's (or dean's) opinion about them. I never want any student to fall victim to being misjudged ever again.

Students are actually in control of their own destinies. If you don't want to be misjudged, you have to understand who you truly are first. But that is only part of it. The other piece is that just because you know yourself better than anyone and appreciate what makes you a unique individual, does not mean you are presenting that exact information to others. We project ourselves on social media, in an interview, during an impromptu meeting with a key influencer, on our résumé, and, yes, on the college application. Those on the receiving end, AOs in this case, make a snap judgment immediately and quickly move on to the next person up for judgment.

Consider meeting someone for the first time, whether it is your parent's boss, an alumni interviewer for a college, or even a potential employer. First impressions are everything. You want them not only to be impressed with you but to *remember* you. It is that latter piece that we sometimes overlook. Most of us are so focused on impressing the person on the receiving end that we forget how important it is to say something powerful and truly distinctive about ourselves. It is easy to get so distracted in that moment that we jumble a few generic words together to describe ourselves before the individual moves on.

All it takes is seconds for someone to judge us. Yet all it takes is seconds to say something profound about ourselves. When we do that effectively, the person on the receiving end comes up with a similar statement about you.

I remember my first television interview after I launched my business. It was with a local news station not far from my home. In the moments before we went live, the news reporter came into the green room and asked me how I would describe myself in the crowded industry of college counseling. I was so nervous that I couldn't even explain what made me different. My words were incoherent. My message was unclear.

I never got asked back for another interview at the local station. But I learned from that moment that if I don't have a message to remember, no one will remember me. And I had to be ready for my next shot.

As I worked on transitioning from forgettable to memorable, I honed my message. TV opportunities force one to do that. If you are lucky, you get about twenty seconds or less to explain yourself on live TV—about the same amount of time you get when you meet an admissions officer at your high school or at a presentation.

I could say simply, "I am America's College Counselor." But in those early days of building my brand, I honestly didn't have enough credibility to just say five words about myself when talking to TV producers and new clients or even speaking on live TV. I refused to be unprepared again. I memorized a version of my Soundbite that could make sense to anyone I met:

> I am America's College Counselor, providing high-quality college admissions advice to all families through monthly Facebook Lives, a weekly blog, and up-to-the-hour responses to the thousands of members of the online community I built, Application Nation.

Thirty-six words in total. Short enough to be said during a TV pitch. Long enough for a stranger to understand exactly who I am. The goal was that anyone on the receiving end, whether in a one-on-one conversation, an interview, or an email exchange, would be able to come away with a similar description of me:

> Sara Harberson is America's College Counselor, offering the highest quality of college admissions resources and advice to all families, regardless of socioeconomic status, to help them succeed in applying to college—YES!

That reciprocal exchange happens in every interpersonal encounter, including the admissions process, whether a student consciously creates his own Soundbite or not. If you don't have a Soundbite or a clear guide to how to approach your application (and life), then it will be hard for an AO to come up with a complimentary and accurate Soundbite on you.

Here's the thing, though. The AO is still going to write a Soundbite after reading your application. Do you want to leave it up to the AO or someone else to determine that for you? Instead, do you want to set the tone for who you are and what your application says about you?

I remember meeting one of my former students when he was just a sophomore in high school. At the time, he was doing well in his classes and about to compete in the National History Day contest. I was so impressed with his project. He was already showing signs of being a budding historian as a tenth grader. I mentioned to him and his parents how it was so unusual for a student to have a clear academic interest so early in high school. That's when the student told me that he didn't want to major in history in college; he was interested in business.

I always respect a student who knows what he wants out of his future, but I also know that mixed messages in an application can lead an AO to inaccurately portray a student in the Soundbite. I know this firsthand. I remember writing Soundbites like this:

> Student says they want business, but the application points toward a history major—DENY.

Or more commonly, when I worked at Penn and many students would try to get into the Wharton School of Business through the "back door," I would write this:

> Student says they want history, but application points toward a business major—DENY.

Knowing this, I knew the student needed a clear Soundbite, one that any AO would be able to glean from his application when the time came. This student was ten steps ahead. He began to invest his time in the business opportunities offered at his high school, like DECA, a popular business club offered at high schools. But he never forgot the stories and "history" of his people and peers. He used his highly effective communication skills to become a two-time national DECA champion. His passion was the intersection between communication and business. From the category he competed in, to the social media platform he built to tell the stories of students like himself, to leading his large high school as the president of student government, his message in his application—his Soundbite—was clear:

> I am a two-time national DECA champ who champions my family's heritage through a social media account on race and my peers as president of student government.

His National History Day achievement graced his application, but it was this greater message of using history to tell stories and affect the marketing and communication of businesses that ultimately took center stage. We will never know what the admissions officer who read his application would have written, but based on what I know, they could have easily written a Soundbite like this:

> DECA national champion (2x!), president of student government, and a champion for his culture make this young man a business leader to watch—ADMIT.

"Admit" is the right word. He was admitted to Penn's Wharton School of Business.

This example reminds us that the Soundbite serves two roles. It is not only how students present themselves but how others, more specifically AOs, view them. The AO's Soundbite on the student will read differently, but it should evoke the same distinctiveness of the student's intentions. When that happens, the AO picks up on the student's Soundbite and the powerful pieces of the application.

Let me be clear, though. The Soundbite is not something a student copies and pastes on her application. Rather, it is a guiding principle that

keeps the student on track in making the best decisions about her life and preparing for the college admissions process:

- What classes she takes
- Which standardized tests she takes and when
- How she spends her free time
- Which teachers she asks for recommendation letters
- What topics she chooses for her essays
- What major she lists on applications
- What colleges she applies to
- Where she ultimately enrolls

The student who is most successful in the admissions process has an application that embodies her Soundbite so effectively that the AO reading her application comes away with a similar statement or Soundbite about her without ever seeing it written. Thus, the Soundbite has a mirror effect. It is the student's defining identity, and it is the AO's defining statement on the student.

In an era when a massive admissions scandal revealed students masquerading as individuals they were not and parents falsifying their children's credentials, AOs want to see proof more than ever that the student behind the application is exactly who she says she is. In other words, the application process is not only about coming up with a catchy Soundbite for yourself. It is about showing evidence throughout high school and in the application to back up the Soundbite.

The Soundbite approach is a way to show authenticity and provide the most convincing and powerful application possible. Leadership roles, honors, and test scores are now verifiable if need be. Admissions officers can follow up with the high school to make sure that the student has truly achieved what she claims. Essays are verifiable too, not only by running them through computer software to ensure they are not plagiarized but also by reviewing the letters of recommendation to ensure that faculty members are backing up the personal qualities coming through in a student's writing. If a student is working off an accurate Soundbite of herself, she has nothing to worry about.

The reason the admissions scandal occurred was because parents believed their children didn't have a strong enough Soundbite or identity compared to others or that their Soundbite wasn't strong enough for the colleges they wanted their kids to attend. We all can acknowledge how damaging it is to a student's psyche when she feels like she cannot measure up—so much so that she or her parents must lie, cheat, or pay off others to get an acceptance. But it also suggests that a student needs to be a top athletic recruit or have a top SAT score to get admitted to college. The reality is that the most successful students are known less for national recognition and high scores and more for the genuineness of their spirit.

Nothing is truer than genuineness. Take a look at the Soundbite of a former student of mine:

Student's Soundbite:

> I am a first-generation Lebanese American who has moved many times, been separated from family, and sacrificed my youth to be able to have that dual identity, and this motivates me every day to contribute to the refugee community I once came from. (Harvard University)

AO's Soundbite:

> This student's remarkable journey to live in the United States fuels his actions to improve the lives of his younger siblings, refugees, and others in need—ADMIT.

The moment I met this young man, I was moved by his story—not the "honors" bestowed on him from organizations or his school, but the honor of being a big brother to his younger sisters and the proud son of immigrants trying desperately to become citizens. His main college essay wasn't about some monumental award he received. Instead, I encouraged him to write about the daily struggles and triumphs he faced to give his sisters a real childhood amid the uncertainty of being forced to leave the United States once again.

AOs don't have to walk in your shoes to be moved by your journey. But you have to be willing to share details of your life, details of your Soundbite, in every section of the application to give it authenticity. When you do that, you will be known not for what others do for you but for what *you* do.

You don't have to be a world-class athlete or a national winner of anything. In actuality, you just have to be a world-class human being. While not every college will admit even the most impressive student, you just need one college to see what you see in yourself.

I have used the Soundbite concept as an admissions officer, associate dean of admissions, and dean of admissions—judging students in a matter of minutes or even seconds by writing a one-sentence statement that defined their admissions decision. But it was not until I became a college counselor at a high school that I realized the Soundbite was something students could control.

The students I worked with as a college counselor didn't have parents who were famous actors or multimillionaires. My students believed they were living ordinary lives, but I saw them as extraordinary. Most of us fall into this category and can easily relate. I needed them to realize what made them extraordinary. I needed to give them the confidence to project it. And I taught them how to live it.

I now use the Soundbite concept with all of my private clients and with the thousands of families in my Application Nation community. It gives students the tools they need to live the best versions of their lives and project that to others. Never again will they be misunderstood or judged unfairly. Instead, their applications are the most inspiring and genuine representation of who they are. Their admissions results are positively startling, especially in this highly competitive landscape.

Soundbite has always been rooted in authenticity. It is about knowing yourself really well. It is about presenting that to others. But the final piece of Soundbite is that you have to live by it. If you don't, others will see right through the facade.

So how do you find your Soundbite? It is within you, even if you haven't uncovered it yet.

CHAPTER 3

The Power of the Soundbite

M ost students believe "decision day" is when they find out they have been accepted to college. But decision day occurs much earlier than that. It is the day when an admissions officer opens up the student's application to read it, recommends an admissions decision, and in some cases makes an "on-the-spot" admissions decision depending on the college's review process. AOs read dozens, sometimes hundreds of applications a day. Your application might be the first one that an AO reads that day, or it might be the last.

As much as the AO must handle these applications with care and understanding, he has a job to do. It is one of the most exacting jobs on the planet, due to not only the limited time he has with each application but the impact he has on a student's future. While most applicants are not even old enough to vote and are still considered to be minors in the eyes of the law, the AO must be objective and detached in the way that judges and surgeons are. AOs carry a student's fate amid the backdrop of an unending number of applications waiting to be read. He wants to be moved by what he reads, but he is often tediously slogging through piles of applications from students who blend in rather than stand out.

The AO is not casually reading through your application. He is methodically going through it, making real and mental notes that highlight how special or unspecial a particular section is. Specialness comes in the form of the pieces of the application. Believe it or not, the student has some or entire influence over their transcript, test scores, recommendation letters (yes, they have influence over these as well!), activities, honors, and essays. The AO will create his own shorthand version, like this, to highlight the details that the college will care about and each piece of the application:

MAJOR: English

TRANSCRIPT: Mostly Bs in "most challenging curriculum" at the school. One C in Honors Geometry in ninth grade; all As in English. AP Language in eleventh; AP Literature in twelfth.

TEST SCORES: Below average ACT, but note the 35 on English section and 36 on Reading section.

RECOMMENDATION LETTERS: AP Language teacher wrote, "Best student of twenty-five-year career."

ACTIVITIES: Only student in school history to be editor in chief of the school newspaper two years in a row.

HONORS: School newspaper won National Scholastic Press Association Pacemaker Award during her junior year.

ESSAY: Wrote about being raised by a single mom through the eyes of her father—mind-blowingly novel approach to a relatively common topic.

But the AO is also paying attention to aspects of the application that are seemingly out of the student's control: race, gender, home address, high school, citizenship, parents' education, parents' occupations, and even if the student is applying for financial aid at a need-aware college. He will highlight, scribble notes, and internalize these pieces on an electronic notecard of some sort as they can reflect institutional priorities.

For example, if the college is trying to attract and enroll more male students to even out the gender balance on campus, this student might have a higher bar to reach in the admissions process. But if the college is trying to increase the number of students from her home state, she might be in better luck.

The AO will have his own way or the admissions office's preferred way to note a student's specialness, or lack thereof, as he quickly moves through the application, section by section. His notes and markups allow him to keep track of the remarkable and unremarkable aspects of the application. He is building a case for his recommended admissions decision. His Soundbite must provide enough evidence to back it up.

The moment he finishes reading the application, he glances through those things he highlighted, circled, or even notated. And within seconds, he must sum up the student in a sentence:

> We have plenty of females applying as English majors, but the student is playing to her strengths as a writer, and it paid off as she might be the best writer in our pool, and she is from a state we need students from—ADMIT.

The statement written by the AO is not a full snapshot of the student's application; it's not even a full snapshot of the notes that the AO wrote about the student! It's a Soundbite. I coined this term to reflect the swiftness of this process. It also acknowledges that the sentence an AO writes is simply a takeaway or defining statement about the student who left an impression on him. That is what sticks out, and that is what dictates the student's outcome. The AO's Soundbite on the student serves many purposes:

- Provides proof that the admissions officer read the application
- Serves as a quick reference for the admissions officer who is handling hundreds or thousands of applications each year and is often reviewing the application several times throughout the cycle for updates, changes, and waitlist activity
- Helps other members of the admissions staff or university community who review the application to understand the most important aspects of the student before or after a final decision is made
- Provides a recommended admissions decision for the AO, the admissions committee, or a senior member of the admissions staff making final decisions

For the longest time, I only saw the admissions process through the eyes of an admissions officer. I summed up students quickly because I had to, and I saw it as a one-sided experience. I was judging them. Before I became a parent myself and felt the protective pangs of a mom, I felt emboldened by my role as an AO. The power I had, even as an inexperienced twenty-four-year-old AO and law school dropout (more on that later!), was shocking. The Soundbites (or bottom lines, as Penn used to call them) that I wrote almost always led to the recommended admissions decision I suggested.

Nowadays, families often share their concern that students have no control over their future based on how the application is treated. But they do.

I had a realization when I started working as a college counselor at a high school and then later as a private college counselor assisting clients. The most breathtaking applications were not necessarily from the students who had straight As or near-perfect test scores but from students who knew themselves incredibly well, made deliberate choices that reflected what was important to them, and were not afraid to be themselves and project that identity to everyone they came in contact with. When that happened, they received more acceptances than they or others ever expected. Unknowingly, they essentially created their own Soundbite and let it guide them through the many challenges and pitfalls of the admissions process.

CHAPTER 4

Evolution of the Soundbite

I am often asked when and how I came up with the Soundbite idea. It came to me during a car ride home from my job as the director of college counseling at a private high school. I took the job because I needed to pivot. I had been home with my three young kids for a few years, and I truly missed being a part of the college admissions process. I was dreaming about it. I was reading every article I could find. And I was even making videos in my parked car in the driveway about it. (Those videos would become the foundation of my first website several years later.) I needed to get myself back into the field.

But commuting three hours a day to work took its toll on everyone in our family. My "mom guilt" was off the charts. My cell phone service was spotty at best, so I couldn't even get work or family calls done on the commute. I started listening to the radio, especially if I could find a long interview with a politician, artist, or celebrity. It made the time fly by on my long commute home and helped me to unpack the stories of the students I had spent my day listening to as well.

I have always loved biographies, interviews, and stories of real people—young and old. It is easy to recognize why I fell in love with the college admissions process. I find inspiration in an individual's candor, challenges, and pivots. But that night on my drive home, I was feeling frustrated. I had spent the entire day meeting with students from different grades, one right after the other. I was trying to remember all of them. They all seemed to run together: premed, prebusiness, pre–Ivy League. Every single one of the students was focused on what they wanted from their future, and none of them were focused on what they were doing at that moment. It didn't mean they weren't doing something special, but the way they described themselves was less than memorable.

I knew better than anyone that unless they began to see themselves differently, they weren't going to see the results in the college admissions process they wanted. As always, I found myself formulating my own quick summary of the student in my mind. That is how I was trained as an admissions officer and how I trained a new crop of admissions officers every year as an associate dean and dean of admissions. The goal in reading an application was to cut through all the pieces of it and get down to the bottom line on each student:

Another premed student—WAITLIST.

Interested in business like so many others—what makes her interest different?—DENY.

> Focuses on getting an Ivy League education, but I didn't get a sense of who she is—DENY.

On that car ride home, I kept changing the channels, searching for some inspiration when I heard a radio host interviewing a popular performing artist. The host asked the performer why he had been so successful in his career. The performer described how his music was something no one had ever made before or since. No sooner had I wrapped my mind around what the performer had said than the host replied something like, "You nailed it. That's your SOUNDBITE."

I was struck by the irony of the moment and the power of one word: Soundbite. The radio soundwaves. The performer who was able to capture his purest identity in a matter of a few words. And the host who had seen and heard everything in a long career spanning decades was so noticeably moved.

I pulled into a rest stop on the turnpike and typed "Soundbite" into the notes app on my phone. It gave meaning to that drive home, the students I was responsible for at the high school, and my own existence at that time. I realized the power we hold in the words we use to describe ourselves.

I returned to work the next day with that one word in my mind. It was so powerful on so many levels. "Bottom line" may have been the term I used when I was reading and making admissions decisions for colleges. As a college counselor at a high school filled with kids who reminded me of my own, "bottom line" felt sterile and abrupt. Soundbite captured what I was doing for years on the college side of the process, but it was a much more student-friendly and, dare I say, human-friendly idea. It made me consider that if students were empowered to identify their own Soundbites, they would dictate not only how they saw themselves but how they were evaluated in the admissions process.

I had the background to help my students. I knew what moved me and what didn't, and my instincts were spot-on after years of coming up with "bottom lines." But it was my own evolving Soundbite for myself that became the tool in getting students to see their own. I was no longer a dean of admissions. I was no longer a stay-at-home mom. I didn't know what my future held. Right then and there, I was a college counselor who had to use every magical strategy I had in my toolbox to give students confidence to do things, say things, and write about things that no one else around them was doing.

When I began working at the high school, I was still fairly new at the college-counseling part of the process. I had spent years judging students from afar. As much as I got to know some students and even their families through the admissions process working on the college side, I tried to distance myself from them when it came time to objectively evaluate their applications. I didn't know the daily struggles they faced. I wasn't aware of the pressure they felt to impress me. I didn't remember how lost I felt in understanding myself at that same age.

The reality was that despite reading applications from students with highly competitive grades and test scores, only a small percentage of them truly impressed me when I worked for colleges. For the students who truly impressed me, I advocated for or signed off on acceptances. If asked what made the difference, I would often say it was their essay or their activities list, but that was an oversimplification of something much more complex. If a student got admitted, it wasn't just one thing. There was a gravitas that was all over the application. Back then, I didn't spend time wondering what exactly separated certain students from the rest of the pool. My allegiance was to the college ultimately, not the student.

All of a sudden as a college counselor at a high school, I had a constant flow of students coming into my office, sharing their highs and lows with me. They came to me when they wanted a hug or a shoulder to cry on and when they needed someone to celebrate the big and small accomplishments of their lives. I began to see students in a different light. I was no longer the judgmental AO formulating a Soundbite in my mind. Instead, I had a new identity—a new Soundbite—for a period of time:

> Mama bear, protector of my students' mental health, supporter of their plans, and advocate for everything that made them extraordinary.

But many of my students didn't see what I saw in them. They were often focused on their weaknesses, how they compared to their classmates, and the past and future rather than the present. I could relate.

Soundbite was the solution. My students were already defining themselves whether they realized it or not. I needed to get them to define themselves differently. If not, admissions officers might have the same problem I'd had a day earlier, being unable to distinguish one student from another. I looked at my notes from the day before:

1. I want to be premed.
2. I am interested in business.
3. I want to go to Harvard (or fill in the blank with another Ivy League school).

These were very common Soundbites. I had heard them thousands of times. There was so much more to these students than what they were saying about themselves. I could see little things I wanted to learn more about. I saw potential in them that they didn't quite see right away. I recognized traits, experiences, and ideas that set them apart rather than made them all run together. We had our work cut out for us.

In our next set of meetings, I started to gently uncover the pieces of their stories that I wanted to hear more about. I encouraged them to do things that they needed a push to do. And I tried to get them to focus less on their limitations and others (classmates, peers, and family members) and more on their strengths and themselves.

The students who defined themselves as wanting to be premed needed to recognize the traits and experiences of their present-day lives that made them the individuals they were. If they were truly taking advantage of these qualities and opportunities every day, others would see it too. That meant that they didn't need to be mini-doctors in high school. And they didn't need to do what every other premed student was doing: hospital volunteering, providing research assistance in a lab, shadowing a doctor, attending a summer program for future doctors. In fact, I wanted them to do something entirely different from what their peers were doing.

What about those students who wanted to major in business but didn't have a reason for it beyond the fact that a parent worked "in business" or they felt that it was the best way to make a good living? Or the students who wanted to go to an engineering school but couldn't explain why? Or the many more students who had no idea what major they wanted and just chose one randomly because it sounded impressive or that was what their parents wanted them to do? They needed to sink their teeth into something that was specific to who they were, and the rest would fall into place, I promised.

And the students who wanted to attend an Ivy League school needed to focus less on the end result and more on the journey. Literally. There were opportunities passing them by because they were focused on this idealized version of college. They saw older students from their high school and older siblings getting into these colleges, and they defined success by getting admitted to an Ivy even if it wasn't the right fit for them.

One of those premed students I was hoping to positively influence was also a golf player—a particularly good one, in fact. She had started playing the sport very late compared to most of her teammates, and she didn't appear to have the typical family background of many golf players. She was a first-generation American and raised by a single mom, or at least that is what I assumed. I had not heard her speak about her father, and he never showed up to the family college-counseling meetings. I was dying to know why.

Admissions officers are the most curious individuals about other people's lives. You could take the AO role out of me, but I would always be that curious individual wanting to know as much as I could about a student. In that moment, though, I would have to settle for what I knew:

> Premed applicant, first-generation American, golf player.

We were getting a bit more specific in our many formal and impromptu talks. I had learned that her mom came from India and was a scientist at a research center in the city. The student told me that she started playing golf in eighth grade. Everyone said it was too late. She was determined to prove them wrong. Getting recruited to play golf in college was a goal for her. We would have to see if it worked out. I gently poked and prodded her to share little things along the way.

When it came time to write her main college essay, there were some obvious topics she could write about: golf, wanting to be a doctor, or her determination. I wanted to know something about her that was not so obvious, though. It took a while for her to open up, but she did.

After some deliberate questions on my part, she explained how she barely knew her father and hadn't seen him in years. When I mentioned that she could write about him, she insisted that she had lived without him for her entire life, and there was no way she was giving him that much of a presence in her application. Good point.

I pushed further. I asked her why she was so determined about everything in her life—golf, being a doctor, not wanting her dad in her essay. She told me it was not to prove to her dad she was worthy of his attention; it was to honor her mother. Bingo. Sometimes we focus on an adjective as a defining trait like "determined," when it is the actions we perform every day that define us in a much more personalized and breathtaking way.

She ended up writing an essay about the challenges, stereotypes, and joy that come from being raised by a single mom. The essay referenced her mom, but the focus was on how she saw herself. And it was beautiful. Every single draft moved me to tears.

And when one day her cell phone rang during one of our meetings after school, she politely asked if she could answer it. Of course, I obliged. I was far more relaxed as a college counselor than I had been as an admissions officer. She excused herself for a few minutes and came back in. I, the always curious former AO, asked what it was about. She shared that her mom had a side business and all the phone calls went straight to her cell phone. She was the frontline of the business. I was shocked. Everyone, including herself, defined her as a golf player. No one knew about this extraordinarily intriguing secret life. She was the receptionist, assistant, negotiator, and saleswoman behind her mom's successful medical research business. I was beyond impressed.

When she was ready to fill out her activities list on her application, I mentioned that she should list working for her mom. She wasn't just pushing papers around. It wasn't like she needed a job just to say she did one for her college applications. Her mom relied on her like a full-time employee. It took some convincing, but she was working a substantial number of hours—much more than a typical part-time job for a high school student.

By the time all of the pieces of her application came together, she was not just a premed applicant, a first-generation American student, or even a recruited athlete. She was this distinctly special young woman who embraced herself to show all the qualities of a future doctor by doing things her way. My notes after reading through her application one last time before she submitted it were as follows:

> Defying odds, she is the daughter of a single mom/immigrant who refuses to rely on anyone for motivation as she manages to achieve at the highest levels in school, on the golf course, and in the field of high-tech scientific advances—ADMIT.

My impressions of her after reading her application led me to a clear vision about what AOs would think of her. I felt confident. I gave her my blessing on her application. She submitted it. My instincts were right. She graduated Phi Beta Kappa from Princeton University with plans to apply to medical school.

One of the many students who had dreams of doing an undergraduate business program also found her Soundbite. Instead of relying on what everyone else was doing, she went out on a limb:

> Perfect business applicant: creator of a blog and website providing girls like her, who want to achieve in school, in their careers, and in their personal lives, with advice and mentorship from female CEOs—ADMIT.

She got admitted and attended New York University's Stern School of Business.

And all those students I worked with then and continue to work with now who are so focused on a certain college, be it an Ivy League university or another name-brand school, I challenge them to ask themselves the hard questions. If they see themselves applying to one of these schools, they need to examine exactly why they are interested in it. Is it just the aura of the place? The reputation? The association? Or is it that they truly understand the curriculum, program, and offerings?

Oftentimes, students will explain why they are interested in a college by repeating what the tour guide shared during the tour, the admissions officer discussed in the information session, or something mentioned on the homepage of the college's website. But those are the reasons and messaging for all, not the individual student. I want my students to wade through the marketing strategies and be able to articulate a real reason for choosing a particular college.

If that doesn't happen, the student has a hard time writing the college's supplemental essays. She ends up repeating the common themes that the majority of applicants mention. The application is less personal and more mainstream. But when a college's acceptance rate is in the single-digits, mainstream doesn't add up to an acceptance for a regular kid. And I can usually predict the outcome of the application when that occurs.

But it's heartbreaking when a student doesn't get admitted to their dream school. Part of my job as a college counselor is helping the students get back on track if that occurs. I remember countless students being devastated after being deferred or outright denied by an Ivy League university in the Early Decision or Early Action round. After the dust settled, we took a look at the rest of their college lists and agreed to invest in making sure that every single college they still had to apply to was on their list for a very good reason. I challenged them to explain to me why a college was on the list. If they mentioned its Ivy League status, reputation, ranking, or common themes, I told them they either needed to investigate that college further or take it off the list. It forced them to remove the perceived Ivy glow of certain colleges and examine their own glow. Their Soundbites shifted from focusing on wanting to go to an Ivy League university to Soundbites that focused on them. When that occurred, they started to cut through the marketing strategies of a college just like an AO cuts through an application and to find the real gems waiting to be uncovered.

Even if the early results weren't what they hoped for, my students ended up seeing incredible acceptances in the Regular Decision round: Middlebury, Johns Hopkins, Wesleyan, UCLA, George Washington University, Bucknell, Wake Forest, Davidson, and the list goes on and on.

Every single one of those students who was initially devastated by not getting into their dream college ended up supremely happy at their destination college. In the end, I believe where they ended up was a better fit for them. It may not have been their dream college initially. But it ended up being a powerful reality in the end.

The reason why all of these stories worked out is because my students were able to create their own distinctive Soundbites, paths, and college lists. Sometimes that happened well before senior year, and sometimes it happened in the midst of it. No matter when the Soundbite comes together, it has an immediate effect on the student and her outcomes. If a student lives and projects a positive, powerful, and distinctive Soundbite, AOs and others will see it and respond in kind. The Soundbite concept works for everyone who is willing to work on him- or herself.

When a student doesn't know where to begin with their Soundbite, I like to give them a mock interview. I have been "interviewing" students since my final year of college when I was one of five senior interns in the admissions office at Hamilton College. Even then, I had a mental list of what questions to ask students to learn as much as I could about them. It came in handy as an admissions officer, dean of admissions, college counselor at a high school, and now as a college counselor *to all*. Thousands of interviews later, I know that if I can't draw relevant information from a student, no one can!

The mock interview is now the most popular option I offer my Application Nation students these days. Not only does it prepare them for a real college interview, but I manage to gather so much valuable information to help them with their Soundbite and identify powerful topics for essays. In one hour, I ask as many questions as I can, gently encouraging them to share pieces of their story, from their culture and ethnicity, to their family, to the activities they do and subjects they love, to the little things about themselves that somehow transform them into world-class human beings. They finish the interview feeling *world-class*. I finish the interview often in tears because of their moving stories and inspired to point out their Soundbites and a half dozen essay topics for them to consider writing about.

I know what AOs want to see and hear about a student. Sure, AOs like students who win national awards. But they also really appreciate the students who win over their classmates, peers, and communities. My questions lead students to take stock and realize they usually don't have to do anything more. They just need to project what they are doing in the most powerful way.

Here is an example of a Soundbite that came from my Application Nation mock interviews:

> I understand the mechanics of biomedical engineering from watching and experiencing my own foot surgery, and my extroverted personality welcomes new freshmen to my school and encourages my male counterparts in AP Calculus to open up, come together, and collaborate.

This student floored me during the mock interview when she shared that she asked her doctor if she could stay awake during her recent foot surgery. I asked her about the hardware used in the surgery, and we chatted about the field of orthopedic medicine through the eyes of a biomedical engineer. That's when I pointed out to her that as a future biomedical engineering student, she had firsthand knowledge of how advances in medical technology can improve healing.

And when she told me she was one of the only females in her AP Calculus BC class, a class especially important for a future engineer, I asked her what role she played. She explained that she drew her classmates out of their shells, encouraging the boys in her class to open up, share, and collaborate for much better results on projects than if they stuck to themselves.

It was no surprise that she was part of the "welcoming committee," formally and informally, in every environment she was in. She officially mentored freshmen in her high school through an orientation program, and she made everyone around her comfortable to share things about themselves that helped her relate to them and helped them relate to others.

The orientation program would be listed on her activities list. She had complete control over how she described her role in that activity. But if her AP Calculus BC teacher saw her draw out her male classmates and achieve something far greater as a group, her recommendation letter would back up her Soundbite. When it came time for her to write about why she was interested in biomedical engineering in her supplemental essays, nothing would be more powerful than explaining how she laid awake during her surgery to watch the steel rods going into her foot to better understand how engineers work closely with medical professionals to improve surgery, healing, and rehabilitation.

And finally, when she shared the extraordinary topic she wanted to write her main essay on, I couldn't contain my excitement. It was about something no one would ever know about her unless she wrote her main essay about it.

Essay Topic:

> What started off as a comedy podcast with Grandmom about her fear of squirrels has taught me that asking the right questions can open doors to learning about my family's history.

Her ability to draw people out not only came in handy in her male-dominated AP Calculus BC class but also allowed her to learn about the stories of her family. Her main essay wasn't about her surgery, biomedical engineering, or her role as an orientation leader at her high school—all of that would show up on her application already. Instead, she wrote about something that her Soundbite complemented. She ultimately made everyone around her feel so comfortable that it allowed her to see, hear, and experience things that are often hidden beneath the surface.

One of my other Application Nation students is known for his science research. He is a published author on oncology and works on his own longitudinal study. But what came through in the mock interview was his ability to use baking and cooking to better understand his own research and the vast academic disciplines that reach far beyond science. Being the oldest of five kids with two working parents provides him a laboratory to create culturally inspired and historically relevant confections in his kitchen for his family, his school, and the essential workers in his community during the COVID-19 pandemic.

His Soundbite reads like this:

> I am a home cook, food blogger, and community activist who uses food and cooking techniques to develop new discoveries in science, humanity, and history.

Some might say his genius lies in his research. But I was most impressed with how he uses food to explain issues far beyond science. During the mock interview, he mentioned creating a final project in AP US History of a multilayered trifle representing slavery, race, and equal rights. I was glad to hear that he chose this teacher to write one of his letters of recommendation. Surely, this teacher would mention this extraordinary project in the letter.

And when he shared with me that he overheard a family member express disappointment in his interest in "girly" activities like baking and cooking, I told him he had his essay topic:

> I haven't always fit into the cultural, gender, and societal expectations of my extended family, but in being a creative, I am changing the expectations for the next generation and inspiring my siblings to live out their dreams.

When students need a little direction on what makes them special, their Soundbite, or essay topics, I tell them to ask the questions I would ask in a mock interview:

- What are you interested in majoring in? How did that interest come about?
- What's been the hardest part of high school?
- What's your favorite keepsake?
- If I asked your classmates, what would they say about you? How would they describe you?
- Describe your parents, siblings, and family.
- What characteristics do you get from each of them?
- Where do you think those qualities come from?
- When have you taken a risk?
- What has been your biggest personal highlight over the last few years?
- Has someone said or done something hurtful to you?
- What responsibilities do you have at home?
- What is something that someone said or did that made a positive impression on you?
- Are you misunderstood?
- Tell me about a moment in your life when you were truly scared?
- Is there something particularly meaningful to you in your room, house, or community?
- What would you want a college to know about you?
- What would I be surprised to learn about you?

The answers to these questions reveal the things that students often hide in their everyday lives; yet they speak to who they are much more than big awards, leadership titles, and perfect grades. This is what AOs want to learn about them.

Not all students are ready for my questions, though. Sometimes they answer them in a very perfunctory way for most of the mock interview. But almost always, even if they do, I can get something profound from them when I ask the last question: What would I be surprised to learn about you?

I don't know if I finally break them down or they realize they can trust me. But when they answer that question, I am so honored. They end up sharing something extraordinary, and that's when I know what makes them special. That's when I know we have their Soundbite, possibly their essay topic, and the essence of who they are.

CHAPTER 5

Be Honest About Your Strengths and Limitations (Self-Awareness)

For years as an admissions officer, I was so focused on writing Soundbites about students. I viewed it as a one-sided exercise where *I* defined the student. It wasn't until I was working with students as a college counselor that I realized that Soundbites work in both directions. I started to recognize that the "regular" students who didn't have any special connection to get them admitted were the most successful when they and their applications seemed to embody a unique description or identity of their own. My students didn't think of it as a Soundbite per se; they just had an underlying self-confidence to pursue their own path and worked on following that path every day. However, that is easier said than done in high school, where everyone wants to blend in instead of standing out.

It takes a lot to be self-confident in high school. As a mom of three strikingly different kids, I have paid particular attention to the students who exude confidence throughout my career. I want my kids to be so self-confident in whatever they love to do that they pursue it so unabashedly because it brings them fulfillment, whatever that is.

The self-confident students typically fall into one of two categories. Either they have incredibly supportive and progressive parents behind them who encourage them not to be afraid to be different. Or the student is so obviously different from the rest of their family, culture, or community, and they celebrate this to the fullest.

It is like that amazing Application Nation student who has such confidence in being one of the only females in her AP Calculus BC class that she has the boldness to enter a male-dominated field like biomedical engineering. Or the other Application Nation student who created a multilayered trifle to signify slavery and race relations for his AP US History project. His parents were the ones who had bought him a KitchenAid mixer several years earlier—because they believed in him and encouraged him to follow his passion. Duly noted.

If you are a student reading this book, I hope you realize right now that if you are so different from everyone around you, seize the opportunity. You won't regret it. Go after what makes you different. And if you are a parent like me, encourage that difference in your child like it's the most important thing you can ever do for them.

I was searching for my own confidence during that first year as a college counselor. I knew how to be an admissions officer, but I was new to the other side of the desk, the other side of the process. So I did what I knew best and quietly observed my students in our meetings, in classes, at sporting events, and in weekly assemblies. Even if that first group of students I worked with didn't consciously write a Soundbite, I had written one for them that I kept to myself. I was not quite sure anyone would believe my secret approach actually worked. But I knew I was onto something, and so were my students.

My students did what I want my own kids to do: they consciously chose to do things differently. They did not choose to be the student who just joined a club because their friends were doing it. If they did, I pointed it out. They didn't say they wanted to major in science because that's what seemed to impress others. They didn't apply to the same colleges because that's what everyone did at their high school. Instead, they possessed a trifecta of traits: self-awareness, intentionality, and storytelling. Each trait worked independently while also complementing the others.

Self-awareness, intentionality, and storytelling are powerful tools anyone can embody at any age. Yet my entire focus is getting young people to tap into them sooner rather than later. Students are far more effective in turning goals into reality when they do.

The first trait in developing your Soundbite is self-awareness. You must be honest with yourself about your strengths and limitations. This is the hardest trait to exercise. We all have it in us to understand ourselves in the most objective and thoughtful way. But in doing so, we must uncover the strengths that others don't see yet and face the limitations that others are quick to point out.

Strengths can be in any area: academics, extracurricular activities, hobbies, and even personal skills. No matter what, the strength is always more interesting and powerful when it is nuanced or specific. Think in terms of being a specialist rather than a generalist.

The specialist carves out his niche and thrives in his own space because there is no one else like him. The generalist has to compete with everyone else: the all-around good student, the athlete, the contributor. There is nothing wrong with being a generalist. In fact, most of us could say we are good at a lot of things. But that's exactly why you want to go one step further.

Instead of trying to compete with hundreds, thousands, or even millions of other people who are strong in that same general area, go deeper to figure out what very specific aspect of that area you truly excel in. There is always at least one thing (and many times more), even if it is very small or inconsequential to some, that opens up a world of opportunity. And when you identify that one thing, you are self-aware and are on the road to becoming a specialist.

Take, for example, the student who excels in a traditional academic subject, like English, math, history, science, or languages. Let's say a student is particularly strong in English. No matter the year, teacher, or class, the student is clearly enjoying herself and performing well to the point that she could easily say English is her best subject.

Okay, that is part of being self-aware: recognizing a clear strength. But remember, the more specific you can get, the more unique your Soundbite becomes. Watch how a strength can go from being general to special:

1. My best subject is English.
2. My best subject is English because I am a good writer.
3. I am actually a comedic writer.
4. I am a comedic writer who is working on a project.
5. I am a comedic writer writing a TV pilot to resurrect the half-hour American sitcom for the next generation.

Millions of students could say that they are strong in English class. Thousands could say they are good writers. Hundreds might be able to identify themselves as comedic writers. Dozens might have enough of an interest that they do some writing on their own. But only a handful or less are actually pursuing this very specific genre of writing and creating a body of work to back this up.

That body of work is your treasure. And you can start working on that treasure at any point—going into high school, going into senior year of high school, or going into the next chapter of your life, no matter what age you are. It is not about reaching the pinnacle of success right now; it is about working on your craft right now.

Some critics will argue that younger children are not always ready to pursue their strength, that they can burn out quickly. I say that pursuing any strength at any time teaches us what it feels like to love something so much about ourselves. And the strength can change over time. No one has to pursue their strength forever, so don't be afraid to give it a try for now.

The strength can relate to a sport or another activity as long as the student is truly setting themselves apart in a much larger pool. It can be as unexpected and nonacademic as being particularly effective at organization and packing or knowing everything there is to know about your state's bird or the history of cars. Or it can show up in interactions with others, like being the person who resolves conflicts between groups and individuals or who speaks perfect, unaccented French despite being a nonnative speaker.

We can be *good* at a lot of things in our daily lives. But finding what we are *exceptional*, even world-class, at is the difference maker. While the strengths that a teenager has will evolve over time, recognizing the things that they do exceptionally well *right now* can give them confidence when they need it the most. The beauty of the Soundbite concept is that a student can be celebrated for both academic and nonacademic strengths.

I love the story of one of my students who would run to and from school every day. Sometimes she would run half the distance and take public transportation the rest of the way. Sometimes she ran the full seven miles. She became an expert at packing just what she needed for the day in her tiny runner's backpack. She had to leave enough time to shower in the locker room before school began, and she had to work efficiently at school in order to take only the books and notebooks she needed home. She faced hecklers on the streets and doubters at her school.

Why on earth would someone do this voluntarily? Because it was her strength at the time. She was known as that kid who did something different, and it made her stronger than anyone else around her. Strengths can be as simple as stamina—physical and mental stamina. She had both.

The other aspect of self-awareness, though, is being able to recognize our limitations. Notice my word choice. I never use the word "weakness" because it implies that we are not good enough. The word "weakness," with its particular meaning, tends to dominate our lives—so much so that it can easily define us. For example, if a strong academic student doesn't do well on standardized tests, often he will harp on that and present it almost as a disclaimer to his counselor, his alumni interviewer, and even his AO. And when that happens, the very thing that he doesn't want to hold him back becomes his Soundbite:

> I don't do well on standardized tests, but I am a really good student.

By seeing his test scores as a weakness rather than a limitation, the student defines himself by what he can't achieve instead of what sets him apart. Anyone who comes in contact with him won't remember that he's a really good student or even an exceptional one. They will only remember that he is not a good test taker. That dominates the student's Soundbite of himself and the person on the receiving end's Soundbite of him.

AO's Soundbite on the student:

> This kid should apply to Bowdoin or another elite test-optional college because his test scores are too low for us, but the rest of his application is phenomenal—DENY.

Using the word "limitation" instead of "weakness" gives us perspective to consider other opportunities right now and the potential to overcome that limitation in the future.

If that same student applied without test scores to Bowdoin, the first test-optional college in the United States, he could be viewed very differently as long as his Soundbite and application highlighted his strengths. The AO's Soundbite could read like this:

> Extraordinary academic record of an extraordinary young man—ADMIT.

Because our Soundbites evolve over time, limitations can become strengths. I think back to my high school self and the lack of grammar, writing, and analysis I did in my local public school. I was unprepared for college writing, and I struggled mightily in being able to write a basic essay, let alone an extended paper, that first semester of college. I initially didn't have the skills or confidence to write. Yet, over the years I honed and perfected my writing, and now I write for a living. Even if our limitations never change or improve, it gives us room and encouragement to focus on our strengths even more. I still have other limitations, but they don't define me.

The exercise for this chapter is called "Know Thyself." It is the motto for Hamilton College, my alma mater. This activity is a tribute to the education I received and what I figured out about myself while I was there. I remember having to register for my first semester of classes as a freshman. Everyone around me seemed smarter and more prepared for what was to come. My fellow classmates were talking about being premed and signing up to take calculus and biology, and all I could think was "Sara, know thyself."

My concept of Soundbite was decades away from development, but I had enough understanding to know that I had no business taking premed classes. I knew my strengths and my limitations too. As much as I wanted to impress others at that time, I knew myself. I signed up for the classes I could handle and thrive in. That inspired me to take theater and rhetoric that first semester and later led to a whole lot of English classes.

The Know Thyself Exercise will encourage you to think broadly and deeply about the obvious and not-so-obvious strengths you have. This is the first of three activities in Part 1, and it will help you prepare for the Soundbite Exercise.

I encourage you to explore multiple strengths in different categories. Sometimes the student's Soundbite ultimately highlights the unlikely connection between two seemingly different strengths. I call this the "special-special" and will elaborate on it in Chapter 13. No matter what, though, pay particular attention to #4 and #5 of the strength categories. One must *enjoy* the strength and truly want to pursue it, at least for the foreseeable future, to use it in the Soundbite Exercise. This is crucial to uncovering your Soundbite as many of us do things for other people instead of following our hearts.

What is also crucial is recognizing limitations but never allowing them to get in the way. The moment you share a limitation with someone else, they remember your limitation instead of your strengths. That means that if you don't do well in geometry in ninth grade, don't feel the need to focus on it. AOs will see the grade on your transcript. There is no need to explain why you didn't do well in it. It just draws unnecessary attention to a limitation.

If you don't do as well on standardized tests as you do in your classes, be smart about your limitation. Apply to test-optional colleges where this won't even be an issue.

If you don't have any traditional leadership roles to report, you don't need to mention that in an interview or have your college counselor explain that in the letter of recommendation. Instead, in interviews and in your activities list in the application, describe the nontraditional yet equally impactful roles you play in the activities you do engage in and the life you live. And do it proudly.

In general, though, I typically do not encourage students or their letter writers to share, write, or explain anything related to the following:

- Learning differences or disabilities (LDs). There is still widespread discrimination against students with LDs in the admissions process, despite this being a federal offense.
- Mental and psychological diagnoses, including eating disorders, ADHD, ADD, depression, and anxiety. As with LDs, AOs are not properly trained to handle these illnesses, and this can lead to a swift denial.
- Lower Advanced Placement scores. AP tests are typically not required for admission. Only share scores that will help you. Sometimes that means only sharing scores of 5, especially if you are applying to highly selective colleges.

Until admissions offices begin to see students who fall into these categories as exhibiting extraordinary strengths rather than limitations, I am very cautious about sharing this information in an application. There are examples of students sharing this in an application and successfully overcoming the bias, but it takes a very special student to do that. While we are protected by the Americans with Disabilities Act, colleges have been anything but compliant and often use a learning, physical, or psychological issue as a reason not to admit a student. So unless you have a foolproof plan that I approve, I would not share it. Many AOs see these examples as limitations, while most of us see them as strengths.

Always lead with your strengths. Always project what you *can* bring to the table rather than what you cannot.

KNOW THYSELF EXERCISE

The Academic Strength

1. Are there any academic classes that you are clearly strong in—meaning that you excel in them in terms of the grades you receive and/or the teacher has made a point to mention your strength in their class?　☐ Yes ☐ No

2. If yes, please list the class, year of high school you took it, and the final grade you received.

   _____

   _____

   _____

   _____

3. Within this academic specialty, was there one area, lesson, or unit you found particularly interesting? If so, what was it? This hints at a specialization within a greater academic discipline!　☐ Yes ☐ No

   _____

   _____

   _____

   _____

4. Did you enjoy this class and exploring this academic area?　☐ Yes ☐ No

5. Do you see yourself pursuing this further outside class?　☐ Yes ☐ No

The Extracurricular Strength

1. Is there something you do in your free time that you have particular strength in? This can be a sport, performing arts, fine arts, a hobby, a part-time job, a family responsibility, or even a special skill set.   ☐ Yes ☐ No

    _____

    _____

    _____

    _____

2. How do you know that you are particularly strong at this? Did you get acknowledged personally by an individual, organization, or your community? If so, list the acknowledgment.

    _____

    _____

    _____

    _____

3. If you have been acknowledged for your personal contribution in some way, was it on the local, state, or national level? Acknowledgment can start with a coach, mentor, or community member who compliments you. It can also be an award, a newspaper article, or recognition by a community or organization—locally or beyond.   ☐ Yes ☐ No

    _____

    _____

    _____

    _____

4. Do you enjoy the activity?   ☐ Yes ☐ No

5. Do you want to continue doing it?   ☐ Yes ☐ No

Personality or Unusual Strength

1. Do you have a personality strength that others have acknowledged? It can be anything from building consensus, to working with certain individuals (infants, children, the elderly, those with certain medical issues), to handling an emergency. This is a tough one to identify, but a lot of times the reason one is successful in an academic or nonacademic area is because of an underlying personality strength. ☐ Yes ☐ No

    _____

    _____

    _____

    _____

2. How do you know it is a personality strength? Did someone tell you, or did an outside organization recognize this? If not, is there a pathway to explore this further?

    _____

    _____

    _____

    _____

3. Have you been recognized through leadership, job, or award opportunities for this strength? ☐ Yes ☐ No

    _____

    _____

    _____

    _____

4. Do you enjoy using this strength? ☐ Yes ☐ No

5. Do you want to continue developing this further? ☐ Yes ☐ No

Remember that even if you are not actively pursuing an unusual strength yet, this doesn't mean you can't start, literally today, no matter what grade you are in or how old you are. You won't regret it, no matter when you begin.

Everything, even being especially skilled at the perfect handshake, small talk, etiquette, table designs, styling, photo editing, video editing, and critiquing old movies in your spare time, can turn into something extraordinary.

While I always want students to focus on their strengths, they need to acknowledge their limitations so they know not to lead with that. EVER.

THE LIMITATION

1. List any and all academic, extracurricular, and personality limitations.

   _____

   _____

   _____

   _____

2. Now that it's out of your system, move on and don't harp on it unless it turns into a strength!

CHAPTER 6

Avoid Following the Crowd (Intentionality)

Identifying strengths allows us to see things in ourselves that set us apart. The more unusual, specific, or nuanced the strength is, the more opportunity there is to pursue it on a grand level. And, frankly, the less competition there is for you at the top. It can be specializing in a specific position in a sport, like the long snapper on the football team. It can be studying a rare theory in math. It can be sewing a certain type of thermal blanket for the homeless. Specialists are special. And although not every team, college, or organization needs *your* specialty, part of life's journey is finding that one team, college, or organization that does!

It takes a lot of guts to go after something unusual, especially in high school. It is sometimes easier to blend in instead of standing out. Peer pressure, bullying, and the human desire to want to be popular can limit us from pursuing what makes us special. In fact, many students join clubs, take classes, apply to certain colleges, or accept a job opportunity because their friends are doing it. This is hard to recognize or admit, but having self-awareness can help us move into our own realm in the future.

That said, it is absolutely necessary to take breaks, hang out with friends, and give yourself time to recharge. Just because you want to do something with your life that no one else is doing doesn't mean you have to give up doing typical things that fulfill you—like hanging out with friends. Sometimes it is important to take a break and do things simply because your friends *are* doing it! I just never want students (or adults) to feel so dependent on their friends that they aren't willing to focus on themselves. Part of being intentional is knowing when to spend time developing your strength and when to take time off from it.

When I worked at a high school as a college counselor, I could easily identify students who focused too much attention on what their friends and classmates were doing rather than what they truly wanted to pursue. The biggest club at the school was Model United Nations. The school was small, but it was hard to find a student who wasn't a member of Model UN.

Coming from a highly selective admissions office at a university and a college, I knew that while this was a wonderful way to engage in simulated policy and diplomatic exercises and meet students from all over the country, it was hard to stand out. Clubs across the country are typically large, and only one student can lead the group each year at least in terms of an official title. The competition is stiff at the national conferences, so winning a big award is difficult.

The high school where I worked was highly academic. Every student went to college, and the higher-ranked colleges carried cachet. Some of the smartest students in the class were part of Model UN. So many students who wanted to be seen as smart joined the club. It didn't matter to them that it may not have played to their strengths. It didn't matter that when challenged a bit, they really didn't have a reason for joining besides the fact that everyone else seemed to do it. And it was such a huge time commitment, with not only weekly meetings but the annual conference at Harvard right smack in the middle of spring semester. Students scrambled to keep up with their schoolwork. The stress to go on this trip while our school was operating on a regular schedule was visible among my students.

If it really meant something to all of those students going, I was all for it. But most of my students were just going along for the ride. They could say they did the Harvard Model UN Conference—but so could the thousands of other students from hundreds of high schools across the country. Did putting Harvard Model UN Conference on an application ever get a student into Harvard or another elite college? The answer is no.

And while it was cool to be smart at the high school where I worked, other high schools value popularity, athletics, or the arts. No matter what type of high school you attend, be aware of this trap. The Soundbite approach is never about what everyone else is doing; it is about the individual path you take that sets you apart.

Every young person, teenager, and adult has followed the crowd at some point, though. It is a dead-end street, and it leaves us feeling unfulfilled, unhappy, and underrealized—until, of course, we pivot.

Thank goodness for the pivot. It holds no prejudice or bias. It can be done by anyone, no matter their race, gender, age, or circumstances. The pivot becomes the most miraculous moment in your life until another pivot comes along to replace it. Pivoting is a strength. Go back and add it to the Know Thyself Exercise!

The pivot has become my saving grace. Several times in my life I followed the crowd instead of my own strengths. We all have those moments, right? During those periods of my life, I felt invisible because I was doing things to please others or because I didn't have the courage to take the less traveled or more challenging path. Sometimes those periods lasted only days. As a high school senior, I thought for a hot second I should apply to a large state university, because everyone around me seemed to be applying there, instead of the small, no-name liberal arts colleges I had on my list. Thank goodness my gut was telling me something. I couldn't sleep worrying that the large state university was not the right place for me. I decided to stick with my original plan.

Other times, going down the wrong path lasted longer. I went to law school—to please others, not myself. When I finally had the guts to withdraw during my second year and agree to pay back all the loans that I had to take out in my own name, I never looked back. Every time I wrote my monthly check to pay off my law school loan, I felt stronger and, dare I say, *richer* in knowing and valuing myself. It was an intentional decision that some people questioned—many, in fact. There was a lot of hard work that followed, including a period of time with no job. But I was committed to the pivot, and it landed me in my first college admissions job at the University of Pennsylvania.

That's the thing about the pivot. It is not about quitting. It is about being intentional with your choices and making sure they line up with your strengths. When we stop using the word "quit" and start seeing the word "opportunity," we realize the power of being intentional with our choices and decisions.

I love working with former dancers, athletes, and actors. They remind me of myself—well, sort of. Technically speaking, I am a former dancer (pivoted away at age eight), former athlete (pivoted away at eighteen), and former actress (pivoted away at age twenty-two). Many of us can relate to pursuing something like the arts or athletics so intensely that everything else around us becomes secondary. Most performing artists and athletes reach a point where they stop pursuing their craft. Sometimes it is because of injury; sometimes it is because of burnout. Not to worry, though. These individuals tend to find their next craft quickly and embrace it just as passionately.

One of my Application Nation students did ballet for hours each day for years. When she got to high school, she wanted to try something else. She threw herself into the school yearbook and learning Italian and got involved with organizations that promoted religious and racial tolerance. She appreciated her years of dance, but she didn't feel bad about setting her sights on other pursuits. As she said during our mock interview, "A dancer is always a dancer, even when she's at the bus stop." It is the qualities of pursuing a craft that stay with you for the rest of your life and fuel you even when you pivot to do something else.

I tell students to "map it out." If you have a goal in mind and it plays to your strengths, map it out in a journal or on paper, poster board, a dry-erase board, a phone, or a computer. I'll show you how to do this and the questions that need to be answered. You should look at your answers every single day, as many times during the day as you need to. This is a way to stay focused on what is important to *you* and not get distracted by others and other opportunities that are not nearly as helpful to you.

By the way, everyone needs to be intentional about their lives. It doesn't matter if you are looking at the most selective colleges or ones with open enrollment. You have goals in mind for your future, and if you want to reach them, you have to be deliberate about what you do and how you do it.

For example, if a student wants to major in engineering, she needs to be intentional about her choices, and the earlier she starts, the better. At the end of the chapter, you'll find the Map It Out! Exercise. It actually matches up with a college application to ensure that you are staying on track.

I have included filled-in versions for three of the most competitive and popular types of majors: engineering (computer science, specifically), pre-med, and business. By looking at the filled-in versions, you can see how to be intentional about every section of the application. I included a blank version for you to fill out based on your own interests as well.

The Map It Out! Exercise is important because if a student has a goal in mind about the type of college and the major they want, they need to make decisions and be intentional about every section of the application. By being intentional, the student can provide extensive evidence to back up their application for that college and even the desired major.

Remember, admissions officers look at a student's intended major before diving into the application. They will be looking for different things depending on the major listed.

TRANSCRIPT

The AO focuses on core subjects first and foremost: English, math, science, history, and a foreign language. I teach my students to try to stick to my "5-4 Plan": all five core subjects for all four years of high school. Elective or noncore classes can be extremely helpful to a student in determining their academic interests, but students applying to traditional four-year colleges should try not to let these classes take the place of core classes.

Elective, noncore classes can be "add-ons." In other words, if the student has room in their schedule to add these elective, noncore classes, they should, as these subjects often lead a student to discover a hidden strength. But among elite colleges, elective, noncore classes may not be factored into the admissions process. Not to worry, though. Those elective, noncore classes in high school can become required classes for a student's major in college. If I hadn't taken public speaking in high school, I may not have pursued communication as my major in college!

STANDARDIZED TESTS

Just as AOs take a quick glance at the student's major before diving into the application, they also take a look at the student's test scores. They know that if the student's scores are below range and the applicant does not meet an institutional priority or come from an underrepresented background or state, the student is highly unlikely to get admitted. The AO may take even less time "reading" the application, knowing that the student's scores are low. I always tell students with lower test scores to be honest with themselves and apply to colleges that will give them a fair shake. That can mean applying to test-optional colleges.

RECOMMENDATION LETTERS

For a selective college, a student's college counselor of record writes one letter of recommendation. Typically one or two letters from core teachers may also be required. Ongoing communication with all your letter writers can ensure they know you well and are up-to-date with what you are interested in. If your academic interest changes over the summer before senior year, make sure all of your letter writers know this!

Talking to and interacting with a teacher outside class well before you ask them for a recommendation letter builds up that relationship and strengthens the letter they write. If one of the teachers writing for the student teaches them in the subject (or a related subject) the student wants to pursue, the letter can provide an added layer of evidence.

ACTIVITIES

Extracurricular pursuits are one of the most enjoyable ways to explore an academic area. To show evidence of their interest, students don't need a full résumé like someone applying for a job in that field. But having a few activities that match up with what they want to major in can provide an opportunity to get some exposure and even hands-on experience in the field.

MAIN ESSAY

The main essay should never be about your goals for college and your career. Save that for your supplemental essays. Instead, your main essay should evoke your best qualities, which you hint at in your Soundbite!

Write the main essay about something that won't come through anywhere else in the application. AOs want to learn something about you that only you can share.

SUPPLEMENTAL ESSAYS

These are additional essays that students may be required to write for individual colleges and programs. Because many supplemental essay prompts are about why a student has applied to that college/major or their most meaningful extracurricular activity, I always want to make sure that students save these topics for the supplemental essays rather than the main essay. Knowing what the prompts are will ensure that students don't repeat themes in their essays. Layering ideas in the application is always better than hammering the same idea again and again!

Instead of following the crowd, follow your strength. And be intentional about what you choose to take, join, pursue, engage in, and spend your time doing. The only way to take a strength to the next level is to pursue it unabashedly. The most jam-packed "Map It Out!" forms translate into the most powerful applications! If you have the guts, no matter how much others scratch their heads, doubt you, or even make fun of you, then you are probably onto something that will change your life and society forever.

Following your strength means that you are intentional about everything you do in your life and you are just as exacting as the AO judging you. In fact, the more intentional you are, the stronger your Soundbite and application will be.

MAP IT OUT! EXERCISE (ENGINEERING STUDENT)

What is your goal for the immediate future? List specific majors, programs, and types of colleges here:

Get accepted to a selective engineering program as a computer science major at a four-year university in the Northeast.

Transcript

- What classes do you need to take to get you there?

  The most advanced-level classes I can handle in all five core subjects for all four years if possible! [By the way, this answer rarely changes no matter what major or program you want to pursue!]

- What subjects are the most important?

  Math and science.

- Which specific classes will the program be looking at?

  AP Calculus AB, AP Calculus BC, or a postcalculus class by senior year.
    One year of biology, one year of chemistry, and one year of physics at the least.
    The most advanced physics class available at the high school by senior year (AP Physics 1, AP Physics 2, AP Physics C: Electricity and Magnetism, AP Physics C: Mechanics).

- What grades do you need to get?

  Strong grades across the board, especially in all math and science classes.

- What elective, noncore classes are helpful to *you*?

  Possibly an "Introduction to Engineering" elective at my high school to make sure I am interested in the field. [While some high schools offer elective engineering-focused classes, these should not take the place of core academic classes. Your cores, especially in math or science, are the best preparation for an engineering program.]

- Is there a specific class that the college will be looking at that you can take in high school for the major you listed that is not already listed?

  AP Computer Science A and/or AP Computer Science Principles, or the equivalent at the high school if these are not offered.

Standardized Tests

- Are standardized tests required? If so, which one will you take? The ACT or SAT?

  Most engineering programs will require the ACT or SAT at a minimum.

- Did you take a practice test in each? If so, which one did you perform better on and feel better about?

  I did better on a practice ACT. Therefore, I plan to take the ACT up to three times between junior year and senior year.

- What scores are the programs you are interested in looking for?

  MIT is my top choice. Their middle 50 percent range for the ACT among admitted students is a 34 to a 36.

- What specific sections of each test matter more?

  The Math and Science scores on the ACT matter a bit more. MIT provides middle 50 percent ranges for the subscores of the ACT as well, which are a 35 to a 36 for the Math and Science sections of the ACT.

- When do you plan to take them?

  I plan to take the ACT in February of junior year, July after junior year ends, and September of senior year to maximize my scores.

- How have you prepared?

  I am working with an online class to cover the content and keep me on track leading up to each test.
  I plan to take practice tests leading up to the actual test.

- If your test scores are not as high as the middle 50 percent range of the colleges you are interested in, have you considered test-optional colleges? If so, which ones?

  It is hard to find colleges with engineering programs that are test-optional, but Worcester Polytechnic Institute is test-optional, and I have already gone to visit and love it!

- What other tests are required or helpful for the colleges you are applying to, and when do you plan to take them?

  I plan to take the AP Calculus AB and the AP Chemistry exams in May of junior year after taking these corresponding classes. While not required by most colleges, a high AP score can show more evidence of my ability in math and science.

  I will consider preparing for and taking the Math 2 and Chemistry Subject Tests in June right after taking the AP exams, as long as my practice scores match up with the scores expected at the colleges on the list. But I know that few colleges require these tests nowadays. So if I don't get a chance to take them or if I don't do as well as I hoped, I typically don't have to share the scores.

Recommendation Letters

- Does your college counselor know about your interest?

  We don't get assigned a college counselor until second semester of junior year, but I have reached out to meet with the vice principal, who is also the advisor to the Technology Club, of which I am a passionate member.

- Have you spoken to a teacher you admire or want to share ideas with whose class you have taken? Did they teach you in a class that matches up with or strengthens your intended major?

  I just met with my Honors Physics teacher for the first time. I wanted to see if he had any out-of-the-box suggestions for exploring the field of physics or engineering during the school year or summer. He had an idea of doing a research project this year and asked me if I could help. [Building a mentor-relationship with your teachers well in advance of the time when you ask them for recommendation letters can serve as a strong foundation for their getting to know you and writing a more detailed and supportive letter.]

Activities

• Are you currently doing any extracurricular activities that match up with your intended major?

I have been a member of the Technology Club at my high school. We provide all of the AV and technical support for our school since we don't have a budget for a professional staff. I hope to run for president of the club next year.

I am hoping that the research project with my Honors Physics teacher materializes and works out. It's already November, so I want to get moving on it!

Regardless of whether the research project comes to fruition, I will return to my summer job with the Geek Squad as a customer representative.

• How long have you been participating in these activities?

I have been a member of the Technology Club since ninth grade.

If the research project with my teacher works out, that will be part of eleventh grade at the very least.

I worked at the Geek Squad last summer and plan to work there again this coming summer.

• And how many hours a week do you commit to each of the activities that match up with your intended major?

The Technology Club ends up being between five and ten hours a week during the school year. I sign up for a daily free period, and I also staff after-school events: set up, troubleshoot, and break down the equipment after the event is finished.

I am not sure how much time the research project entails just yet. If it doesn't work out, I have a potential idea, and I could see myself working on it during weekends too.

I worked forty hours a week last summer at the Geek Squad. My boss told me I could have the same amount of hours this summer too.

- If you currently don't have an activity that matches up with your intended major, which clubs, jobs, or other opportunities do you plan to join, start, or pursue right now?

Even though I have up to three potential activities already, if the research project doesn't work out, I have an idea to pursue myself!

The Main Essay

- Did you start a list of essay topics for your main essay yet?

Being raised by a single mom and realizing we don't need a "man of the house" to make important decisions and keep our household intact.

The ethical, personal, and safety considerations of the "bystander effect" and how instinctual it is for me to leap into action after once needing a bystander to help me.

The meaning of the pillowcase on my bed that is fraying and faded, yet signifies a distinct moment in my life that represents the meaning of home.

The Supplemental Essays

- If any of the colleges on your list require supplemental essays, take a look at them (even if you are not a senior) to get a feel for what is asked. List a sampling here.

  One of the MIT prompts: Although you may not yet know what you want to major in, which department or program at MIT appeals to you and why?

  One of the Duke prompts: If you are applying to the Pratt School of Engineering as a first-year applicant, please discuss why you want to study engineering AND why you would like to study at Duke.

  Worcester Polytechnic Institute prompt: WPI seeks students who are the right fit for its academic and campus community. In what ways are you the right fit for the distinctive educational and campus experience that WPI offers?

MAP IT OUT! EXERCISE (PREMED STUDENT)

What is your goal for the immediate future? List specific majors, programs, and types of colleges here:

I want to major in science and be premed at a large public university in my state.

Transcript

- What classes do you need to take to get you there?

  Try to take advanced-level classes in all five core subjects if possible as most premed applicants become students in the college or university's liberal arts undergraduate program.

- What subjects are the most important?

  Science and math classes from ninth grade on.

- Which specific classes will the program be looking at?

  Biology, chemistry, physics, and calculus.

- What grades do you need to get?

  As, if possible, especially in science and math classes.

- What elective, noncore classes are helpful to you?

  Classes for future medical professions like CPR, first aid, Honors Research, anatomy and physiology, biochemistry, and "Spanish for Healthcare Professionals."

- What elective, noncore classes are important to the colleges?

  The core classes matter most!

- Is there a specific class that the college will be looking at that you can take in high school for the major you listed that is not already listed?

  AP Biology, AP Chemistry, or AP Physics (or the equivalent to these advanced-level classes).

Standardized Tests

- Are standardized tests required? If so, which one will you take? The ACT or SAT?

  Yes; I plan to take the ACT since my strongest sections are in math and science and I get a separate score for them to show off my strengths.

- Did you take a practice test in each? If so, which one did you perform better on and feel better about?

  Yes; I did better on the practice ACT.

- What scores are the programs you are interested in looking for?

  The middle 50 percent range for admitted students at my dream school, the University of Michigan, is 32 to 35.

- What specific sections of each test matter more?

  Math and science since I want to be a science major/premed.

- When do you plan to take them?

  Twice in junior year and a third time, if needed, in the summer or fall of senior year.

- How have you prepared?

  I am taking a weekly online course, doing all the necessary homework assigned, and doing practice tests once a month.

- If your test scores are not as high as the middle 50 percent range of the colleges you are interested in, have you considered test-optional colleges? If so, which ones?

  Yes; there are a number of smaller colleges and a few universities in my home state of Michigan that are test-optional if my scores are not as high as expected.

- What other tests are required or helpful for the colleges you are applying to and when do you plan to take them?

  AP exams are not required, but I know that if I do well on them, especially in math and science, they can show further evidence of my ability to succeed in a premed curriculum.

Recommendation Letters

- Does your college counselor know about your interest?

  Yes; my college counselor knows that I want to be a doctor someday.

- Have you spoken to a teacher you admire or want to share ideas with whose class you have taken? Did they teach you in a class that matches up with or strengthens your intended major?

  My Honors Biology teacher from ninth grade is my AP Biology teacher in eleventh grade. I've done well in her class, but she doesn't know me as well beyond that. I should reach out to her and see if she is willing to talk to me about being a biology major in college. This could begin a series of conversations that I have with her well before I ask her for a recommendation letter.

Activities

- Are you currently doing any extracurricular activities that match up with your intended major?

  I am a certified junior EMT in my community. I am also a member of my school's HOSA (Health Occupations Students of America) club, where I compete in the Emergency Medical Technician category.

- How long have you been participating in these activities, and how many hours a week do you do them?

  I just became certified as a junior EMT this year, but I hope to work several shifts a week for my town's EMS squad. I have also been in HOSA since ninth grade. We meet weekly for several hours; the hours increase leading up to competitions. I plan to continue doing both activities through senior year.

The Main Essay

- Did you start a list of essay topics for your main essay yet? If so, list your topics here.

I thought about writing about being a big brother and taking care of my two much younger siblings after school while my parents work.

I also could write about a special wilderness trail I like to hike on my own near my house.

I could write about our family tradition of waking up really early every Sunday morning to drive to my grandparents' farm three hours away. I used to dread it because I just wanted to sleep late like most of my friends, but now those weekly visits have become my most cherished memories and lessons thus far.

The Supplemental Essays

- If any of the colleges on your list require supplemental essays, take a look at them (even if you are not a senior) to get a feel for what is asked. List a sampling here.

University of Michigan:

Everyone belongs to many different communities and/or groups defined by (among other things) shared geography, religion, ethnicity, income, cuisine, interest, race, ideology, or intellectual heritage. Choose one of the communities to which you belong, and describe that community and your place within it.

Describe the unique qualities that attract you to the specific undergraduate College or School (including preferred admission and dual degree programs) to which you are applying at the University of Michigan. How would that curriculum support your interests?

MAP IT OUT! EXERCISE (BUSINESS STUDENT)

What is your goal for the immediate future? List specific majors, programs, and types of colleges here:

> I would like to attend an undergraduate business program at a nationally known university.

Transcript

- What classes do you need to take to get you there?

  I know that I need to do well in all of my core classes.

- What subjects are the most important?

  Math!

- Which specific classes will the program be looking at?

  AP Calculus (or the highest-level math offered or taken).

- What grades do you need to get?

  I should get As in math. Math should be my strongest subject.

- What elective, noncore classes are helpful to *you*?

  Accounting, "Introduction to Business," marketing, entrepreneurship.

- What other classes are important to the colleges for this major?

  AP Economics (if offered) and possibly AP Statistics (but I know that AP Statistics should NEVER take the place of calculus for business majors).

Standardized Tests

- Are standardized tests required? If so, which one will you take? The ACT or SAT?

    Yes; I plan to take the SAT.

- Did you take a practice test in each? If so, which one did you perform better on and feel better about?

    Yes; I performed better on the SAT.

- What scores are the programs you are interested in looking for?

    My top choice right now is Indiana University's Kelley School of Business, and the university's middle 50 percent range of SAT scores for admitted students is 1180 to 1380.

- What specific sections of each test matter more?

    The Math section of the SAT will matter a bit more than the "Evidence-Based Reading and Writing" score for business programs.

- When do you plan to take them?

    Junior and senior year.

- How have you prepared?

    I'll be using a study guide and taking practice tests on my own.

- If your test scores are not as high as the middle 50 percent range of the colleges you are interested in, have you considered test-optional colleges? If so, which ones?

  Yes; there is a growing number of test-optional colleges, and I am excited to explore these as well.

- What other tests are required or helpful for the colleges you are applying to, and when do you plan to take them?

  I have heard that taking the Math 2 Subject Test could be helpful for business programs, but it's not required. I plan to take the AP Macroeconomics and AP Microeconomics exams at the end of junior year.

Recommendation Letters

- Does your college counselor know about your interest?

  No. I changed my mind recently, so my college counselor still thinks I want to be premed. I know I need to tell her my academic focus has changed to ensure that her letter of recommendation for me matches up with the intended major I list on the application.

- Have you spoken to a teacher you admire or want to share ideas with whose class you have taken? Did they teach you in a class that matches up with or strengthens your intended major?

  My AP Macroeconomics/Microeconomics teacher is also my soccer coach. He is the person who got me interested in this field as we talk about business on the bus to and from away games. I hope to ask him for a letter of recommendation when the time comes.

Activities

- Are you currently doing any extracurricular activities that match up with your intended major?

  I am the treasurer of our class, and I have a part-time job during the school year and summer working at one of the supermarkets in my town.

- How long have you been participating in these activities?

  This is my first year as treasurer of the class, but I hope to continue in this role throughout high school. I have been working at the supermarket since ninth grade.

- How many hours a week do you commit to each of the activities that match up with your intended major?

  I usually have one to two hours a week for my role as treasurer. I work ten to fifteen hours a week at the supermarket during the school year and about thirty hours a week during the summer.

The Main Essay

- Did you start a list of essay topics for your main essay yet? If so, list your topics here.

The meaning of my last name and how it defines who I am.

The time I accompanied my younger sister to her freshman year dance because she didn't want to go alone.

The Supplemental Essays

- If any of the colleges on your list require supplemental essays, take a look at them (even if you are not a senior) to get a feel for what is asked. List a sampling here.

  Indiana University's supplemental essay: Describe your academic and career plans and any special interest (for example, undergraduate research, academic interests, leadership opportunities, etc.) that you are eager to pursue as an undergraduate at Indiana University.

MAP IT OUT! EXERCISE (BLANK VERSION)

What is your goal for the immediate future? List specific majors, programs, and types of colleges here:

_____

_____

_____

_____

Transcript

- What classes do you need to take to get you there?

_____

_____

_____

_____

- What subjects are the most important?

_____

_____

_____

_____

- Which specific classes will the program be looking at?

_____

_____

_____

_____

- What grades do you need to get?

  _____

  _____

  _____

  _____

- What elective, noncore classes are helpful to *you*?

  _____

  _____

  _____

  _____

- Is there a specific class that the college will be looking at that you can take in high school for the major you listed that is not already listed?

  _____

  _____

  _____

  _____

Standardized Tests

- Are standardized tests required? If so, which one will you take? The ACT or SAT?

  _____

  _____

  _____

  _____

- Did you take a practice test in each? If so, which one did you perform better on and feel better about?

  _____

  _____

  _____

  _____

- What scores are the programs you are interested in looking for?

  _____

  _____

  _____

  _____

- What specific sections of each test matter more?

  _____

  _____

  _____

  _____

- When do you plan to take them?

_____
_____
_____
_____

- How have you prepared?

_____
_____
_____
_____

- If your test scores are not as high as the middle 50 percent range of the colleges you are interested in, have you considered test-optional colleges? If so, which ones?

_____
_____
_____
_____

- What other tests are required or helpful for the colleges you are applying to and when do you plan to take them?

_____
_____
_____
_____

Recommendation Letters

- Does your college counselor know about your interest? If not, set up a time to discuss this. And if you don't have a counselor or your counselor doesn't have time to meet, whom can you speak with at your school who can be an advocate for you? (Gifted coordinators, International Baccalaureate advisors, principals, and assistant principals can all fill the "counselor" role at a high school if there is not an official college counselor.)

  _____
  _____
  _____
  _____

- Have you spoken to a teacher you admire or want to share ideas with whose class you have taken? Did they teach you in a class that matches up with or strengthens your intended major?

  _____
  _____
  _____
  _____

Activities

- Are you currently doing any extracurricular activities that match up with your intended major? This can be a school club, internship, hobby, or other opportunity. You can have multiple activities that point to your intended major. One to five is a good target!

  _____

  _____

  _____

  _____

- How long have you been participating in these activities? The more years of high school, the better!

  _____

  _____

  _____

  _____

- How many hours a week do you commit to each of the activities that match up with your intended major? The more hours, the better!

  _____

  _____

  _____

  _____

- If you currently don't have an activity that matches up with your intended major, which clubs, jobs, or other opportunities do you plan to join, start, or pursue right now?

  _____

  _____

  _____

  _____

The Main Essay

- Did you start a list of essay topics for your main essay yet? If so, list your topics here. I recommend at least five viable topics to choose from. It doesn't matter if you are a ninth or twelfth grader in high school—it's never too early to start writing ideas or topics down for your main essay. These are just possibilities. The writing takes place once junior year is done. If you are applying to a selective college, do not write your main essay about your intended major. There will be supplemental essays that will serve that purpose. Your main essay can be about something in your Soundbite (as long as it doesn't show up somewhere else in your application), or it can simply just complement it!

_____

_____

_____

_____

_____

_____

The Supplemental Essays

- If any of the colleges on your list require supplemental essays, take a look at them (even if you are not a senior) to get a feel for what is asked. List a sampling here. While they may change by the time you apply, this is a good way to have a sense of what you will be asked to write about in the future. If any of the college's supplemental essay prompts are about your intended major or program listed on your application, this is the perfect place to talk about your academic interests—from a class that sparked your interest, to a teacher who encouraged you to explore this field, to an activity you do. Save it for this essay!

_____

_____

_____

_____

_____

_____

_____

CHAPTER 7

Be Willing to Tell Your Story (Storytelling)

One of the most important aspects of the Soundbite concept is being both an advocate and a storyteller for yourself. Without it, your Soundbite will never have the power to transform your identity. It is like knowing how special you are but not telling, sharing, or showing anyone. For a less communicative or more reserved student, this is the toughest part. But there are so many ways to *tell* your story. It can be as concrete as mentioning your Soundbite in response to one of the most popular interview questions posed to students: "Is there anything else you want the admissions committee to know about you?" Or it can be subtler, like a photographer sharing in her application a portfolio of images of the unusual life she lives.

Storytelling serves two functions. First, it ensures that each section of the student's portion of the application embodies their Soundbite, from the transcript, to test scores (yes even that!), to recommendation letters, to the activities list, honors list, essays, and interview. Second, it makes sure that everyone who is advocating for you understands you, your story, and ultimately your Soundbite.

Let's see it play out.

Many students get why it's important to keep their Soundbite in mind throughout high school. It keeps them on track. But they often wonder how it can benefit their application.

Your Soundbite should be something you look at, turn to, and get inspired by every single day. It keeps you in check. Are you living it? Are you still committed to it? If the answer is yes, you should make it a part of every decision leading up to the admissions process and every decision in filling out the application. Here's how.

TRANSCRIPT

Does a document with classes, grades, and sometimes even class rank tell a story about the student? It sure does. Admissions officers formally evaluate the transcript first, and they typically spend the most time on this section of the application—even more than on reading your essays! And because the transcript carries the most weight in the admissions process, it often can dictate and dominate an AO's Soundbite for the applicant.

But if the student's transcript is not as strong as they had hoped, all is not lost. While highly selective colleges are looking for near-flawless transcripts, both in terms of taking the most challenging curriculum and getting the best grades, there are plenty of colleges (thousands in fact) that will be more forgiving.

One of my students several years ago had a fairly average curriculum and average grades. Yet she was at the forefront of a growing musical trend, not only performing but producing music. She ended up submitting the extensive musical supplement required for New York University (NYU) Clive Davis Institute of Recorded Music.

NYU is currently one of the most selective colleges in the country. Yet within each university, the undergraduate schools are looking for different types of students. This results in AOs looking for slightly different things in an application, depending on which program or undergraduate school the student applies to. While the Clive Davis program at NYU is highly selective, just like all of the undergraduate programs at NYU, the admissions committee can be more forgiving of a student's transcript if her musical talents are exceptional. And my student fell into this category. She was admitted to this one-of-a-kind undergraduate program.

Ensuring that your college list matches up with your transcript is critical, though. You don't want to apply to a list of colleges that expect perfection if your transcript is less than perfect. However, be open to your strengths because there are plenty of colleges that will focus on them much more in the admissions process.

The AO is looking at a lot of things on the transcript. They look at trends in your course selection and grades. For example, they are looking to see if the student gradually added more challenging classes each year. They might wonder why foreign language got dropped from the student's schedule in tenth grade. Or they may circle or highlight lower grades the student received.

AOs are also evaluating the transcript (and every part of the application) in terms of the type of college they work for, keeping the student's academic interests in mind. For example, if the AO works for a college that only requires two years of a foreign language, dropping Spanish after tenth grade might not be a big deal. But if the college recommends at least three years of foreign language (and most highly selective colleges prefer all four years!), not having Spanish in eleventh and twelfth grade could become part of the AO's Soundbite on you:

> One of the best applications this year for the Arts & Sciences program; yet the student stopped taking Spanish in tenth grade, and there was no scheduling conflict mentioned—WAITLIST.

That's why it is so important that your class choices and grades are driven by your strengths, Soundbite, major/program choice, and colleges on your list. When that happens, the AO begins to see a story unfolding from the very start of the application. And sometimes, despite everything else in the application, the transcript guides the AO to write a Soundbite like this because they know how important this piece is to the process:

> Student wants to be a business major, but he chose not to take math his senior year, and he got a C in precalculus in eleventh grade—DENY.

But when the story being told on the transcript matches up with the student's Soundbite, strength, major/program, and college, the AO could write a Soundbite like this:

> This student has taken every advanced-level English class offered by the school, including the electives in creative writing and journalism, and has gotten an A+ in every one of these classes, which bodes well for her intended English major—ADMIT.

TEST SCORES

Yes, even the tests you take, when you take them, and the scores you get tell a story. Is it the story you want AOs to come away with, though? Most students just sign up for standardized tests without thinking them through. They don't take the time to determine whether the ACT is a better test for them than the SAT, or vice versa. But they should. Colleges have no preferences between the two tests, so why not take the test you are better suited for?

But there is an unspoken (and sometimes spoken) philosophy among AOs that the student should take the ACT or SAT no more than three times. After that, it is rare for the score to increase, and it can send one of two messages. Either the student is so focused on getting the highest score possible that they keep taking the test, or the number of tests taken suggests that these scores are more important to the student than anything else in their application. Taking each test requires extensive preparation, which is not something quantifiable, like an extracurricular activity, in the admissions process. In other words, no matter how much studying a student does for the ACT or SAT, it is not something reported on the application.

As much as AOs want the highest scores possible, they want to see an almost effortless pursuit of standardized tests, with the student doing what they need to do and moving on to other more meaningful pursuits. Otherwise, repeated testing (more than three times) drives the AO's vision for the student. The AO's Soundbite on the student can translate into "serial test taker" instead of "serious match."

This student took the SAT six times instead of really committing to something beneficial to those around him—DENY.

It's a tough predicament for the student to be in, given the fact that colleges put more weight on standardized test scores than they let on. But that's why I like students to determine a tentative schedule for when they want to take each test. It can always change. You can always pivot.

If a student wants to try to take the ACT or SAT up to three times, he should spread the tests out to give himself time to prepare, time to take the test, time to take a break, and time to get geared up again. A student who takes the October, November, and December SATs during junior year has a very different story to tell than a student who takes the SAT in December and March of junior year and then once again in August. I rarely see significant improvement in scores when a student takes standardized tests back to back. Scores tend to improve more significantly with a healthy break between each test!

It is true, though, that for most colleges, students don't have to share all of their scores. As long as your high school doesn't secretly list all of your scores on the transcript (please check!) and the college doesn't require all scores, the student can hide how many times they took the test or even hide a really low score.

However, when the rubber meets the road, test scores matter. As much as AOs try to downplay their importance, they play a significant role in the admissions process for colleges that require them—almost as much as the transcript. And just like the transcript, scores can drive an AO's Soundbite like this:

> ACT composite is solid, but his Science and Math scores are lower, especially for a premed applicant—WAITLIST.

Or this:

> Student's Math score on the SAT is below our middle 50 percent range, but her 800 on the Evidence-Based Reading and Writing section is phenomenal—ADMIT.

But testing doesn't stop there for most students. A handful of highly selective colleges still recommend Subject Tests. As it is harder to find a college or program requiring these tests nowadays, I recommend that the student only send or share Subject Test scores when the scores are extremely high and match up with the student's high ACT or SAT scores. Scores from Subject Tests can tell a story too.

If the student wants to major in biology and takes the Math 2 Subject Test because they know how important math is for a premed student and they take the Biology Subject Test, that could provide evidence to back up their intended major. However, if the scores are low and are provided to the college, even if they are not required, they could negatively impact the AO's admission decision. Therefore, make sure your Subject Tests and the scores match up with the colleges you are applying to and the major you list if possible.

> Student got a 760 on the Biology (Biology Molecular) Subject Test and wants to major in biology—ADMIT.

AP scores can also be a part of the mix if you want them to be. If a student takes an AP class, they typically take the AP exam. In some cases, their high school requires this. While many students feel obligated to share all of their AP scores with colleges, they are typically *not* required for admission. They usually come into play well after the admissions office hands over the student to the college's dean of students or advising program, at which point the student may want to get advanced standing or college credit for their AP scores. However, most students share their scores in their applications whether or not they will be helpful.

> Student plans to major in biology but got a three on the AP exam—DENY.

Getting a three on the AP Biology exam as an intended biology major at a highly selective college may hurt you even if the AP score was never required. Make sure that if AP scores are not required, you only share what will help you tell your story, convey your Soundbite, or provide evidence of your intended major!

And if standardized tests are not your thing, not to worry. It is important that you pivot and consider different colleges where your scores are competitive or test-optional colleges where scores won't be required. There is no reason to let test scores define your Soundbite, process, and future.

ACTIVITIES

One of the most powerful ways to get your Soundbite across in your applications is through your activities list. It can tell a beautiful story if you let it. Once you have your Soundbite in mind, the goal is to weave a story and imbue the tenets, takeaways, and qualities of your Soundbite in the way you list and describe each activity. If your Soundbite embodies certain qualities about you, then you want to make sure that your activities back it up. And if your Soundbite projects a certain academic interest, your activities should tell the story of how you landed where you did.

Student's Soundbite:

> As the oldest of six kids, I am known as the "baby whisperer" in my neighborhood, meaning that I can settle any crying or fussy baby with a technique I created.

This Soundbite could come through simply in the student's activities list. She wouldn't have to have all activities point to this Soundbite, but I could envision her listing the following:

- Neighborhood babysitter
- Newborn nursery volunteer at local hospital
- Blog writer on babysitting for those just getting started and those who need tips along the way

It is not just doing activities that match up perfectly with your Soundbite or intended major. It is about showing how the qualities and skills you gained through these experiences speak to a greater message about who you are.

For example, the student who wants to major in business but doesn't have traditional business activities could pull out and highlight the financial, leadership, or mathematical skills they use in non-business-related activities:

> I created Give Me Liberty, a nonprofit organization that connects local businesses to raise money and solve social and economic issues facing my hometown of Liberty.

This student could list that he created Give Me Liberty on his activities list. He could also showcase some of his other activities, which may not appear like traditional business activities but showcase the business-savvy skills he has gained. And just listing a role is not enough. The student should choose his descriptions carefully to tell the best story about himself.

The following are examples of how roles, organizations, and descriptions can tell a story using the limited number of spaces/characters on a college application's activities section. The Common Application allows for 50 characters to list the role, 100 characters for the organization's name, and 150 characters to describe what you do. Don't waste a character.

If you are telling a story about your less obvious business skills, get specific. Don't just list that you are the vice president of your religious organization if there's more to it.

Make what you do clear:

> Role: Fundraising Vice President
> Organization: Young Judaea Youth Group

And for the description, don't write something generic that anyone could say:

> Description: Attend weekly meetings, help organize events and fundraisers, and participate in annual conferences.

Tell a story about exactly what you do. You can say a lot in 150 (or 149) characters, as in the description below:

> Description: Created the group's largest fundraising event, Mitzvah Mensches, which raised $10,000 in 2020. Our club raised the most money of any group in the US.

Or what about the common membership to the school's community service club? You could list something like this:

> Role: Member
> Organization: Triton High School Key Club

Or this instead:

> Role: Chair of Marketing Committee
> Organization: Triton High School Key Club

Most AOs know what Key Club is. Yet most students would write something generic for the description:

> Description: I am a member of my high school's community service club, Key Club. I attend weekly meetings and participate in service projects.

But here's how to tell your story as long as it is accurate:

> Description: Represent the club on local/national TV. Built website and communication campaign, which translated into doubling fundraising & partnerships.

And students often do not list activities that they perform for the family, even though they are just as powerful and sometimes even more influential than a school club. For example, if the student does the family's taxes every year, they should list it! Take a look at this role and the description that follows:

> Role: Tax Expert
> Organization: Brown Family of Five
> Description: Since 9th grade, I organize and prepare my family's federal/state taxes. I identified exemptions and saved my family over $5,000 a year.

Remember, tell the story of how your activities speak to who you are. Don't let others tell it for you.

ESSAYS

We have already touched on essays a bit in the previous chapter's Map It Out! Exercise. But there is no section more ideal to tell your story than the essays. It is a chance to speak directly to the AOs. What will you say? Does it complement the message you are trying to send?

The main essay is a chance for the student to infuse their writing with the qualities that harken back to their Soundbite. Some students write about something in their Soundbite, while others simply write an essay that hints at their Soundbite. Either way, as long as the main essay is about something that is not mentioned anywhere else in the application, it tells a new story, and the AO is instantly more intrigued.

That means essays about activities listed on the activities section are usually not as strong. And essays about stories that your letter writers mention are not as strong either. It is not about hammering one thing home. It is about layering pieces of your story, Soundbite, and life throughout the application. When that occurs, the AO is much more likely to advocate for you.

Your main essay can be about something you experienced or something you carry with you. The possibilities are endless, and the essay prompts are incredibly open-ended. So choose your topic wisely.

I make all of my private clients and Application Nation students choose their topics for their main essays carefully. I know that the topic is just as important as how well written the essay is. AOs get tired of essays about common topics. I encourage my students to write about something that meets my "Essay Topic Rules":

1. My topic puts me in a positive light.
2. There is natural adversity built into this topic to show my growth or self-awareness.
3. No one else could write about this topic.
4. This topic won't come through anywhere else in my application (like the activities list, honors list, recommendation letters, etc.).
5. My topic supports my Soundbite because it directly references something in my Soundbite or hints at it.

If a student meets all of these rules, the topic is usually strong and one that I approve of.

But anyone who knows me well will tell you how much time I invest in the student's picking the right topic. After reading hundreds of thousands of essays in my career, I know what will work and what won't.

A young man I worked with several years ago wanted to apply to college as a junior. There are plenty of colleges that consider applications from high school juniors, but it takes a very special student to overcome the odds of admission with one less year of evidence. The University of Southern California (USC) used to have a special admissions process for these students. If they enrolled in the USC program, they finished their high school requirements for graduation and began their undergraduate work a year early. But whether a college has a designated program for these students or throws them into the general freshman class, it is nearly impossible to get admitted one year before your peers do. I knew we had a steep mountain to climb. And unlike typical high school seniors who have a list of colleges they are applying to, this student only had one college on his list that year: USC. He had only one shot.

When we were selecting the topic for his main essay, I wanted to make sure that his Soundbite came through in the most authentic and transformative way. Yes, he had a really cool "special-special" interest in environ-mental studies and film (Chapter 13 will discuss this). But that was going to show up in a lot of areas in his application. What few knew was that he had an unusual upbringing, which made him incredibly mature and self-sufficient. His Soundbite was as follows:

> Living on my own has given me courage to do things that no else is doing, like when I took my video camera to the southeastern states by myself and filmed a documentary on deforestation.

While most bystanders would tell a student like this to write about the documentary he made for his main essay, that's the proverbial pothole you want to avoid. Why? Because the student's most influential activity (like all of the student's activities) shows up front and center on the activities section of the application and often serves as inspiration for letters of recommenda-tion and possibly even supplemental essays.

But the true purpose of the student's main essay—the one usually sent to all or most of the colleges on the list—is to share something much less obvious. In fact, the more you reveal about yourself that isn't already rep-resented in other parts of your application, the more intrigued the AO be-comes about you.

For this particular young man, I wanted to make sure that his self-suf-ficiency and maturity came through in his main essay to ensure that the admissions committee knew he was ready to go to college one year earlier than his peers. It is one thing for a teacher or his counselor to say he is self-sufficient and mature. It is a whole lot more powerful when the student shows it himself.

In the end, he wrote his main essay about having to take care of himself while his parents traveled back and forth to their homeland on a regular basis. The essay was a tribute to what it was like for him to essentially live on his own, and it moved me to tears. If the USC admissions committee had any doubts about his being able to handle college one year early, that essay sealed the deal. He got admitted and headed off to USC a year before his classmates.

Supplemental essays offer an even bigger opportunity to expand on your Soundbite. The topics for supplemental essays should absolutely be distinct from the topic of the main essay. They can, however, complement each other. In fact, that's what I recommend that you do. Whether your Soundbite is more academic or nonacademic in nature, this is your chance to explain how you will bring personal distinctiveness to a college's campus.

The young man who went to USC after his junior year of high school had an interest not just in filmmaking but in documentary filmmaking on environmental issues. Notice the specialization! USC's supplemental prompts have changed over the years, but one of the prompts when this student applied was as follows: "Describe how you plan to pursue your academic interests and why you want to explore them at USC specifically. Please feel free to address your first- and second-choice major selections."

My student had plenty to discuss in this type of essay, given the fact that he had experience in both film (his first choice) and environmental studies (his second choice). In fact, I call it the "special-special" when a student's Soundbite actually brings two different strengths or interests together. He had a special-special, and it took his Soundbite and application to the next level!

And for those of you whose Soundbites are nonacademic in nature, this is a chance to connect what makes you special to that particular college. For example, the student who sews blankets for the homeless could connect her volunteer work to an existing organization at the college she is applying to or explain how her work could benefit the community there.

INTERVIEWS

Talk about storytelling! Sitting down with an AO or an alumni interviewer is one of the best ways to tell your story. When students want to know what questions they will be asked in an interview, I tell them it depends on the interviewer! But one thing is for sure: if you have done some research on the college and the major you plan to list on your application in advance, and you have your Soundbite at the top of your mind, your answers will show how special you are and how you fit into the college you are interviewing for.

When answering questions, think back to the Know Thyself and Map It Out! exercises, your activities and experiences, and, of course, your Soundbite, which you are about to write right after this! When you do that, your story will flow naturally, and you will set the narrative instead of leaving it open for the interviewer to misjudge or portray inaccurately in the interview report they write for you.

RECOMMENDATION LETTERS

Storytelling feels less in your control when it comes to recommendation letters. Students don't get to see the letters that are written for them when they apply. How on earth can you ensure that your letter writers are telling the story you want them to tell?

It first starts with what you can control: which teachers you pick for your recommendation letters. Most selective colleges will ask for at least one letter of recommendation (and sometimes two) from an academic core teacher. This teacher should teach the student in a core class: English, math, science, history/social studies, or a foreign language.

The grade in which the teacher should have taught the student varies from college to college. Typically, junior year teachers are ideal as they had the student for a full year leading up to the admissions process. However, sophomore year teachers are usually acceptable, and now some colleges are permitting senior year teachers to write for students as well. I would just caution students to be careful with asking senior year teachers for letters of recommendation if they plan to apply to an Early Decision, Early Action, or Rolling Admissions program. And all students should consider an Early Decision program or at least a number of Early Action and Rolling Admissions programs to create some "early" options. These applications are often submitted in the early fall of senior year, which means that the teacher has only a few weeks or a few months to get to know the student before having to write a letter for them.

When deciding which teacher to ask for that letter of recommendation, consider one of my five criteria for choosing the right teacher. Numbers 1 and 2 are absolutely essential, but adding numbers 3, 4, and 5 can strengthen the letter and your application:

1. Have I done well in this class?
2. Am I a strong enough presence in the class that the teacher knows me well?
3. Have I approached the teacher outside class to discuss specific lessons that interest me, seek out mentorship, or share ideas? (Asking a teacher for a recommendation should not be the first time a student speaks to this teacher outside class! The more interactions the student has with the teacher, the better they know the student. It also gives the student an opportunity to share their strengths and Soundbite with the teacher over time.)

4. Does the teacher have a sense of my Soundbite or what makes me special? This can come through in conversations with the teacher in and outside class and in emails.

5. Does the teacher's academic discipline match up with or complement my intended major? If not, have they seen my skills or talents for this major in or outside class?

As most AOs are reading your application in the context of the major/program you are applying to, it is sometimes helpful to have a letter written from a teacher who had you in a class that matches up with or complements the academic interest listed on the application. It is usually not necessary for the letter to come from a teacher in the discipline you want to pursue, however.

The student who wants to major in biology could ask their AP Biology teacher or another science teacher, especially if they had biology as a ninth grader and won't have AP Biology until senior year.

The student who wants to major in communication or a noncore subject in high school may wonder what to do, though. I encourage these students to look for teachers in areas that are closely linked to what they want to major in. For example, a student who wants to major in communication could easily ask an English teacher who can discuss her verbal and written skills in their class.

But a letter can also come from a teacher in another academic area who had the opportunity to see the student excel in the area they want to pursue.

For example, that student who wants to major in communication might have reason to ask her precalculus teacher from junior year because he saw her exhibiting her strength—the ability to communicate effectively—on a daily basis. Maybe that student would break down complex math problems on the whiteboard and explain difficult concepts to her class. This math teacher could highlight her strength and further her Soundbite in his letter of recommendation.

If a second letter from a core teacher is required, the student should go through the criteria for choosing a letter writer once again. Just make sure that you don't pick another teacher from the same core academic discipline, even if both are from the discipline you want to pursue in college. AOs want to see range and dimension in your academic abilities as most colleges have academic requirements that span all disciplines.

Now that you have picked your core teacher or teachers, it is time to ask them. But there's more to it than most students think. If you want to set the narrative rather than letting someone else do it, you need to be willing to share your story at different points in the process.

STEP 1

Reach out via email to your teacher by the spring of junior year. Make it clear that you are hoping to set up a time to formally request a letter of recommendation. This provides a heads-up to the teacher. If they have already agreed to write for too many other students or don't feel comfortable writing for you, this is a chance for them to decline instead of writing a less-than-powerful letter for you.

STEP 2

Set up a face-to-face (or virtual) meeting outside class. Review your Soundbite, moments in class that inspired you, and the reasons why you are asking this teacher for a letter of recommendation. This helps you organize your thoughts before the meeting and allows you to control certain messaging and promote who you are.

STEP 3

After meeting with the teacher, follow up to thank them for agreeing to write your letter of recommendation. In the body of the email, you can reiterate a version of your Soundbite, the transformative lessons and moments from the class that made an impact, and why you asked this teacher. Be aware that anything you put in writing could be copied and pasted in the letter written for you, so you want it to be accurate, honest, and powerful.

STEP 4

At the beginning of senior year, reach out to the teacher via email at the very least to thank them for writing once again. This can serve as a thank-you and a gentle nudge. Include your message and story once again, and let them know anything that has changed.

The other letter that may be required is the counselor letter. This can cause great anxiety for students, as most attend high schools where they have limited interaction with their counselor. The difference between teacher and counselor letters is that the student gets to choose which teachers they ask to write for them. When it comes to the counselor, that person is assigned to the student. For students who attend large public schools, the counselor may not even know who the student is.

The good news is that it's rare for a letter to be negative. Counselors who don't know their students very well will rely on basic information like the student's transcript or test scores, which is already represented in the application. Sometimes they will ask the student to provide a résumé in order to help them write the letter of recommendation. This is not as helpful as it sounds, as the counselor often repeats the student's activities and honors, which will be represented on the application already.

To avoid a basic or redundant letter, I recommend providing the counselor with information that they don't have about you. Make clear for them the following:

1. Biggest academic strength? And what is your specialization within the field?
2. Biggest nonacademic, personal strength?
3. Family background (if relevant)?
4. A version of your Soundbite? (Make sure it's different from the ones you present to teachers writing for you.)
5. Academic major listed on the application (if consistent across all applications)?

Providing this information verbally and, even more importantly, electronically allows the counselor to understand the story you are trying to tell. As I mentioned earlier about the communication to teachers writing letters for you, make sure everything you write is accurate, honest, and powerful, as counselors, especially the ones with large caseloads, often reuse what you say about yourself, almost verbatim.

But if anything changes or you end up applying to different programs, depending on the college, you need to let your counselor know. Or else, this can happen on the AO's end:

> Student's counselor indicates that he wants an undergraduate business education; yet he is applying as a liberal arts applicant, which makes me question his intentions—DENY.

And if your counselor and teachers request that you and your parents fill out what is commonly known as a "brag sheet" to help them write their letter for you, this is a chance to tell your story as well. Just be aware that if your counselor and teachers ask you to fill out a similar form or ask similar questions, you need to provide different examples and answers so that all of your letters don't sound the same. Remember that it's not about hammering home one idea or theme. It's about offering a variety of anecdotes and details that hint at or complement your Soundbite so that the AO on the receiving end understands your story and writes the kind of Soundbite on you that you are hoping for!

Sharing your story is important not only in the pieces of the application over which you seemingly have more control but even in the pieces that you are relying on others to deliver. Counselors, teachers, and interviewers almost always write something positive. But you want them sharing the right message and the right Soundbite. If not, the AO will have a hard time resolving the mixed messages or, more commonly, will not be able to make a strong enough case for admission because your influencers haven't.

You cannot rely on others to tell your story; *you* have to be the storyteller. It can feel forced at times to share aspects of your life and what you do. But that is a huge part of the admissions process, and it is part of getting what you want out of real life too—from finding a job, to securing a loan, to getting investors for your company.

Your story is ultimately the longer version of your Soundbite. You won't need to squeeze every last thing that you are proud of into your Soundbite. That's what the application is for. Let your application tell the story you have always wanted to share.

STORYTELLING EXERCISE

1. Transcript: Do your courses and grades complement your Soundbite or strengths, major/program listed on the application, and colleges on your list? ☐ Yes ☐ No

2. Standardized tests: Do your tests and test scores back up your Soundbite or strengths, major/program listed on the application, and colleges on your list? If not, for which colleges on your list will your test scores be competitive or which colleges offer test-optional policies? ☐ Yes ☐ No

   _____

   _____

   _____

   _____

3. Activities: Are there specific activities listed that back up your Soundbite? If not, are you able to pivot and see how some of your current activities use qualities and skills that indirectly back up your Soundbite? And if not, what activities can you begin doing that will provide the evidence you need? ☐ Yes ☐ No

   _____

   _____

   _____

   _____

4. Essays: Does your main essay hint at or mention the qualities and skills mentioned in your Soundbite? Do your supplemental essays, especially the ones for certain colleges and pertaining to the major you are interested in, speak to your Soundbite? ☐ Yes ☐ No

5. Preparation for the interview: What is your Soundbite? What specific major interests you at this college? What aspects of the college (academic or nonacademic) attract you? How does your Soundbite match up with what the college offers?

_____

_____

_____

_____

6. Recommendation letters: Do all of your letter writers know a version of your Soundbite, what makes you special, why they are writing for you, and what types of colleges or majors you are interested in?   ☐ Yes ☐ No

CHAPTER 8

A Time and Place for Soundbite

When I first begin to introduce the Soundbite concept to a new group of Application Nation families or even a private client, I often get asked the same question: "Where do I list my Soundbite on the application?"

My answer is the same every single time:

You don't list your Soundbite on a college application.

It is not something any college asks for explicitly. It's almost like a secret power. Your Soundbite should be something you generally hold close to the vest as it needs to inspire you every single day, help you in making decisions, and guide your admissions process. If you are living your Soundbite, you actually don't have to tell anyone outright what it is. It should be obvious by your choices, actions, and behavior. However, there are a few times when sharing versions of your Soundbite can help you, like when you are communicating with letter writers or an interviewer, as I mentioned in Chapter 7.

Here is a guide to where to write your Soundbite and when to share it:

It is key to see your Soundbite in writing on a daily basis. It serves as a reminder of who you are and how you want to live your life. While the Soundbite can be shared at times, it is important in this early stage that the student visualizes it privately before they are ready to share it openly. I recommend that once a student writes their Soundbite, they should tack it up on their bulletin board in their room, put it above their mirror, write it in their journal, type it into their phone, and maybe even make it their screen saver on their phone. It should be a touchpoint for the student. If they intentionally come back to it every morning, every evening, or multiple times per day, it will become their mantra. The more a student writes out their Soundbite, says it, and lives it, the more committed they are to it. Seeing it on a regular basis is critical to making it a daily commitment, especially in the early stages. Initially having it visible to only him- or herself can help a student adjust to it and ensure it is absolutely accurate.

The one thing you want to remember about a Soundbite is that it evolves over time. As we become more self-aware, the Soundbite changes. Sometimes the Soundbite becomes tighter and even more powerful; sometimes the Soundbite changes significantly because our interests shift. It is never set in stone. So make sure wherever you write it or post it, it can be easily tweaked or replaced. In other words, painting it on your bedroom walls might not be a great choice, as your Soundbite might change sooner than you think. But making a poster board of it and hanging it above your bed will do the trick, as it can easily be taken down and replaced if and when your Soundbite evolves.

Even though I don't want students plastering their Soundbite on their application, I want their statement about themselves to be present during all of their big decisions. I encourage students to have their Soundbite (and Map It Out! Exercise) with them when they pick their classes for the school year. Students need to be reminded of what is important to them and what they need to do to reach their goals.

The Soundbite should be visible or easily accessible at all times when doing homework. It will help students prioritize their assignments and keep their eye on the ball.

The Soundbite (and Map It Out! Exercise) should be right by their side even when registering for standardized tests. Students should take the tests they need. If a test is not necessary or does not match up with their goals, a student should not waste their time. I would rather see them spending time doing things that allow them to truly live their Soundbite rather than take tests that are not necessary.

One of the best ways to ensure you are following your Soundbite is to keep it in mind when building and finalizing a list of colleges. One of my favorite students in recent years would type her Soundbite at the top of every college list she shared with me, from her starter list to the final one. It was like she wanted to make sure that every college she considered and applied to, and ultimately the one she enrolled in, would value her Soundbite.

When filling out the application, especially the activities section, I want every student to look above their desk where their Soundbite is hanging or look at the Post-it at the top of their computer screen that states their Soundbite clearly and legibly. It should influence which activities to list, their order, and how they are described. There is nothing more helpful in filling out the activities section than a student's Soundbite. It will keep the student focused on making sure they are projecting themselves in the most powerful and distinctive way.

That same student who used to type her Soundbite at the top of her college list would also type her Soundbite at the top of the document she used to write draft essays. It was never copied and pasted into the application. Instead, it was just for her own eyes to remind her of what she valued and who she was. This was brilliant. If she ever lost sight of her Soundbite when drafting the dozens of essays she had to write, she could always come back to it at the top of her document.

I have used this same approach myself. In the throes of book writing, it is easy to get distracted by the demands of daily life. In addition to being a mom of three kids, a wife, and a business owner, I had to find time, motivation, and inspiration to write this book because it is the best representation of *my* Soundbite. How could I not? Every time I came back to the draft of my manuscript, I pulled out a simple folded-over piece of paper that listed my Soundbite, and I propped it up like a little placard next to my computer screen to remind me why I was writing this book. I needed that reminder to keep me focused on who I was.

The Soundbite is ever-present when the student is coming up with ideas for the main essay. The student does not have to write their main essay about their Soundbite. But many times it complements their Soundbite or illuminates a trait or experience present in it. Just like the Soundbite, the topic for the main essay should be incredibly self-aware, intentional about what is shared, and an example of the best story a student could tell about him- or herself, which means no one else in the world could write that same essay in the end! (Appendix C includes examples of my students' Soundbites and essays.)

The Soundbite can be especially useful when writing supplemental essays. It is not required, but many students' Soundbites reflect an academic passion or interest that they have. Other times, the Soundbite ends up celebrating their most important extracurricular activity. Either way, most of the supplemental essays that students may be required to write need to be about why they are applying to that particular college, why they are choosing that particular major, and what activity they are most likely to pursue in college. Having that Soundbite at the top of their minds will ensure that their essays reflect the values, academic offerings, and extracurricular passions that they and the college share.

But sometimes students can be much more explicit about their Soundbites. Here's when they can pull those Soundbites out, share them, and use them to their advantage:

Back in Chapter 7, I discussed the need for students to share with their teachers why they are asking them to write a recommendation letter for them, what they are interested in, and how that class/teacher influenced them. Teachers want students to think through this request as the letter takes time to write, and teachers typically do not get paid extra for recommendation letters.

Most students would find it a bit awkward to end that conversation with "Oh by the way, here's my Soundbite." But how do you ensure that teacher is going to remember all of the details you discussed? Put it in writing! If you have multiple people writing for you (teachers and a counselor), make sure to share different versions of your Soundbite with each letter writer so that the details don't get repetitive.

One of the most important and effective strategies in making sure that the letter of recommendation is as accurate and detailed as possible is to follow up after the formal request with an email thanking that teacher for writing the letter and reiterating the stories, skills, and memories that you hope will end up in it.

Take a look at the following example. Can you spot the student's Soundbite? It might be worded slightly differently than if she were being asked directly by an individual, but it is clear that she is making a bold statement (and a highly unusual one for a high school student) about what she wants to study in college. More importantly, she articulates what she is actively pursuing right now. That's the secret to making a powerful Soundbite!

Dear Mr. Smith,

I want to thank you again for writing my letter of recommendation for my college applications. As you know, I am interested in double-majoring in math and history. For a math-focused student like myself, I had no idea that two seemingly disparate fields could complement each other. However, AP US History became a defining moment in my education. I realized in your class last year that history wasn't about memorizing facts; it was about using numbers to understand the stories of individuals I so desperately wanted to honor.

The discussions we had and the papers we wrote inspired me to participate in National History Day. My research project for this competition examined the untold stories of the women behind the Equal Pay Act of 1963 and how decades later the gender pay gap is still being addressed. This experience led me to uncover my ultimate passion: **quantifying and predicting historical events using mathematical modeling.** It is my hope that the college I end up attending will allow me to study the intersection between math and history as a way to predict our future. Thank you for believing in me and for writing my letter of recommendation.

Sincerely,

[Student's Name]

There is so much wonderful content that this teacher could utilize in writing this student's letter. And a version of her Soundbite is also included.

Just remember that if you write your Soundbite in that email follow-up the same way to every teacher and your counselor, you are going to have letters that repeat things again and again. The Soundbite concept isn't about hammering the Soundbite home in a way that makes the admissions officer want to cringe every time they see it demonstrated in the application. Instead, it is all about layering. So this same student should have different reasons for asking her second teacher to write for her. It may or may not be a teacher who lines up with what she wants to study. However, the student can effectively provide distinct stories and reasons for asking that teacher while also providing variations of the Soundbite to ensure that this second letter gives more dimension to who she is.

Providing different stories and a variation of the Soundbite in each follow-up email to the teachers and college counselor writing for the student will give the AO a wonderful array of examples that all point to the student's Soundbite. Students never should repeat the same message to all their letter writers. The AO wants to uncover something new about you with every section and every letter of the application.

This is a reminder that if the student has to fill out the same questionnaire for each letter writer at the high school, make sure the responses are always reflective of the Soundbite while also being distinctive. The same approach should be used if parents are asked to fill out a "brag sheet" for the college counselor. At many high schools around the country, brag sheets are a way for parents to have input in the counselor's letter of recommendation and to ease the demands on the counselor. What the parents write about should evoke the student's Soundbite but should offer up different stories and anecdotes than what the student has presented already. Layering ideas and stories instead of hammering the same ones allows the student's application to transform itself into something the AO has never seen before.

Finally, just as the AO's Soundbite on the student can sometimes be the "last word," students can have the last word as well. At the end of a student interview, AOs and alumni interviewers often ask, "Is there anything else you would like the admissions committee to know about you?" This is when students rarely know what to say. In fact, many will just reply something like this: "No, I think I covered everything." Or possibly a response like this: "Hmm. I can't think of anything." That is a missed opportunity.

If a student has kept their Soundbite in mind every day, lives by it, and lets it guide every part of the application, including the interview they are in, they will know it by heart. When asked if there's anything else they want to share, the student can confidently state their Soundbite or a version of it out loud, as many of their responses during the interview would have backed it up. There is nothing better than ending the interview with your Soundbite.

Your Soundbite becomes your secret power. It transforms your daily life. If you use it as inspiration and a guide to your application process, the AO will come away with a very similar statement about who you are without you ever having to state your Soundbite verbatim.

There is a time and a place for sharing your Soundbite with others. In the meantime, write it out for yourself, hang it up in your room, and look at it when you get up in the morning, right before you go to sleep, and when you need to be reminded of just how special you are. If you live your Soundbite, it naturally comes through in your application, and you should never have to write it out in the application as a result.

PART 2

CRAFTING YOUR

SOUNDBITE

CHAPTER 9

Get to Work on #lifegoals

Just like a college essay, the Soundbite takes time to brainstorm, write, and edit. But once it is written, it is easy to embrace as long as the student stands by its authenticity. Just as we all change over time, the Soundbite is meant to evolve throughout adolescence and the many chapters of adulthood. It can get better and better as you develop a deeper understanding of yourself.

Let me be clear, though. The Soundbite cannot be written without self-awareness, intentionality, and a willingness to tell one's story. These three tenets mentioned in Part 1 ensure the student has the wherewithal to live by their Soundbite. If students are having trouble talking or thinking about themselves, I would encourage them to return to my favorite mock interview questions, listed in Chapter 4. The student can write down answers to these questions or have a parent or mentor ask them to simulate a real interview. Even if a student is only willing to answer these questions on the surface, the people close to them can draw them out.

Last year, when one of my Application Nation students was having trouble opening up and coming up with strong topics that reached my high standards for a deeply personal essay, the student's mom signed him up for a mock interview with me. The mock interview went well over the allotted time as I asked every single one of my go-to questions in the hopes the student would finally open up. It never happened. No matter what questions I asked, he either gave me a standard response or told me he didn't have a good answer for me. I knew there was more to this student, but he just wouldn't reveal anything beyond the obvious.

A day later, when the recorded video call was available to download, I sent it to the student's mom. I record all of my mock interviews with students because it can be helpful in preparing for a real interview, but it can also remind them of the feedback I gave them for essay topics. This mom sent me an email to thank me for the mock interview. She appreciated the time I took and the endless questions I asked. She also revealed several things about her son that were so incredibly enlightening. The things she shared would make unbelievable essay topics and could strengthen his Soundbite. While he wasn't ready to share them with me, his mom knew him almost as well as he knew himself.

Sometimes parents can gently suggest things that they see in their children that their children don't see yet or may need a little prompting to recognize. Remember the parents who gave their son a KitchenAid mixer from Chapter 5? Thank goodness those parents did that for their son because our world will be a better place for it.

Without a Soundbite, a student's application and an individual's future remain less defined and harder to actualize. It doesn't mean that without a Soundbite you will always fall short; it simply means that if you have a powerful Soundbite, you will *never* fall short.

As you prepare to write your first version of the Soundbite, consider that it is not about putting every last detail into it. One must choose carefully which details to include or, better yet, share. Every single word matters.

This chapter includes the Soundbite Exercise I use with the families I work with. Like you, they hear about the Soundbite concept, but it feels abstract before they actually begin working on it. To get started, consider all of the possible details that *could* be included in a Soundbite:

- A student's unusual upbringing, culture, or homelife, which has shaped who they are
- Academic interest, as long as it's very nuanced or highly unusual
- Special and significant recognition (academic or nonacademic) as a high school student
- Something in which the student shows exceptional promise (academic, nonacademic, personal, etc.)
- Active pursuit or evidence of an interest or passion

The flexibility of the Soundbite is that it is not limited to academics. What makes a student special can be anything: academic, extracurricular, personal, interpersonal, athletic, artistic, behavioral, and so forth. Part of the challenge students face is making sure that those on the receiving end value it.

In this context, those on the receiving end are admissions officers. However, it starts earlier than that. Students should have a list of colleges that will respond in kind. Part 3 will address this further. This same approach can be applied as the student enters adulthood. Aligning themselves with companies, organizations, and groups in their personal and professional lives ensures that they will be recognized and valued as employees, volunteers, and members.

We all just need one opportunity at a time—one college acceptance, one job offer, one mentor. That's right. Just one opportunity is all we need. When we recognize that, we will not get bogged down with accumulating lots of opportunities that miss the mark. Instead we will be focused on the environment that will serve us and our Soundbites best. This is especially important when it comes time to pare down the college list. It is not about applying to as many colleges as possible; it is about applying to the colleges that will value the student.

If being self-aware, intentional, and a great storyteller are #lifegoals, then let's get to work. Remember, though, the Soundbite is not something one casually does in a few minutes. It takes time, multiple iterations, and some soul-searching to do it right. First up is my Soundbite Exercise. I have included a filled-in example and a blank one to fill out. Parents can certainly fill this out for their child and even themselves, but it is essential that the student ultimately fills it out as well!

SOUNDBITE EXERCISE (EXAMPLE)

1. Is there anything unusual about your upbringing, family, or life that has positively or negatively impacted you? If yes, please describe.

    I come from a long line of Quakers that dates back to the 1600s. Quakers have always believed in peace and equality, and those tenets are how I was raised.

2. If the unusual aspect was negative in any way, is there a silver lining in it that reflects who you are right now?

    When some people at school find out I'm a Quaker, they don't know what that means. They are usually not judgmental. I use this as an opportunity to explain my background and the qualities that Quakers stand for.

3. List one, two, or three academic or professional interests that you have.

    Religion and women's studies. But I am not sure what profession I want to go into right now.

4. What classes, grades, test scores, or outside experiences *back up* the interest(s)?

    I attend a secular, traditional high school, so religion classes are not offered. But I am very involved with our Friends Meeting House, which is where we worship as Quakers. I also volunteer at a historical site offering tours. And I took a class called "Feminism in the 21st Century" at my local university the summer before senior year. I got an A in the class.

5. Do you have a very specific focus within one or more of these academic/ professional interests that you have pursued or hope to pursue? Explain.

Yes, I am interested in studying the role females have played in religious communities, including leadership roles.

6. Have you garnered special recognition in any academic or nonacademic areas?

I received the University of Pennsylvania Book Award at the end of my junior year. I am also a member of my school's state championship field hockey team, but I'm not a starter on the team.

7. List one, two, or three things that you do outside academic work in which you show *exceptional* promise.

I like to think that I'm an exceptional big sister to my two younger brothers, who are ages three and four. In fact, every day after school, I pick them up from daycare and keep them entertained, fed, and bathed before my parents get home from work.

8. Based on your exceptional promise in one or more areas, what have you done to explore and develop this further?

Besides babysitting, I haven't really done much to explore this. However, the time I spend taking care of my brothers is significant enough that I plan to list it as a family responsibility on my activities list.

9. If you could pick the most powerful words (nouns and verbs only) to describe yourself, what would they be?

Quaker, Feminist, Big Sister, Equalize, Peace.

10. If you had to write the most powerful, positive, and distinctive sentence to describe yourself right now, what would it be? This is Soundbite 1.0!

    I come from a long line of Quakers, which instills in me a desire to seek equality in society, and I actively pursue this in my research on women and religion.

11. What should you do in the near future to further substantiate this Soundbite?

    I would like to continue to work on my independent research project examining the roles women play in religion and using the Quakers as a model for other religions to follow.

12. Does the Soundbite evoke the answers to #1 through #9?

    Yes, I believe so.

13. Could any other student have the same exact Soundbite as the one you created? If yes, how could you tweak it to ensure it is as distinctive as possible?

    No. I believe my Soundbite is truly unique!

SOUNDBITE EXERCISE (BLANK VERSION)

1. Is there anything unusual about your upbringing, family, or life that has positively or negatively impacted you? If yes, please describe.

   _____

   _____

   _____

   _____

2. If the unusual aspect was negative in any way, is there a silver lining in it that reflects who you are right now?

   _____

   _____

   _____

   _____

3. List one, two, or three academic or professional interests that you have.

   _____

   _____

   _____

   _____

4. What classes, grades, test scores, or outside experiences *back up* the interest(s)?

   _____

   _____

   _____

   _____

5. Do you have a very specific focus within one or more of these academic/ professional interests that you have pursued or hope to pursue? Explain.

_____

_____

_____

_____

6. Have you garnered special recognition in any academic or nonacademic areas? Special recognition could be from an end-of-year awards ceremony at the school or an outside organization.

_____

_____

_____

_____

7. List one, two, or three things that you do outside academic work in which you show *exceptional* promise. This can be anything from playing a sport on a national level to how you treat your elderly grandmother who lives with you. Nothing is off-limits as long as it's appropriate to share with others!

_____

_____

_____

_____

8. Based on your exceptional promise in one or more areas, what have you done to explore and develop this further?

_____

_____

_____

9. If you could pick the most powerful words (nouns and verbs only) to describe yourself, what would they be?

_____

_____

_____

_____

10. If you had to write the most powerful, positive, and distinctive sentence to describe yourself right now, what would it be? This is Soundbite 1.0!

_____

_____

_____

_____

11. What should you do in the near future to further substantiate this Soundbite?

_____

_____

_____

_____

12. Does the Soundbite evoke the answers to #1 through #9?

_____

_____

_____

_____

13. Could any other student have the same exact Soundbite as the one you created? If yes, how could you tweak it to ensure it is as distinctive as possible?

_____

_____

_____

_____

Bravo for completing this exercise! Proudly write your Soundbite 1.0 right here:

_____

_____

_____

_____

If you are feeling good about your first attempt, I will be showing you how to strengthen it further. If you are not sure about your Soundbite just yet, not to worry. This exercise is just to get you started. Your final version will guide you through every step of the admissions process. It will also allow an admissions officer or anyone on the receiving end of your application to see what you see in yourself.

Intrinsic to the Soundbite concept is an unending supply of self-love, self-appreciation, and undeniable motivation. Your Soundbite should move you to do something extraordinary right now, every day. When that happens, the recipient (the AO in this case) is so moved by what you are doing that they reciprocate with advocacy in supporting your application. The rest of Part 2 is devoted to the five rules of writing a distinctive, powerful, and positive Soundbite.

CHAPTER 10

The Soundbite Rules

RULE #1: FIRST PERSON, PLEASE!

I can always tell when a parent or another adult has done a little too much for the student in the admissions process. As an entry-level admissions officer over twenty years ago, I was trained to know when someone else besides the student had filled out the application or written the essays. When I became an associate dean and later a dean of admissions, it was my responsibility to train newly hired admissions officers to do the same. Parents can be incredible brainstormers, editors, and cheerleaders. But now more than ever, it is fundamental that the student take ownership of this process.

Sometimes it's obvious that someone other than the student was involved, like when the parent mistakenly signs their name on the application to verify authenticity (how ironic!) instead of the student's name. Sometimes it's subtler, like when there are two spaces instead of one following each sentence of the student's essays. Yes, that's right! Admissions officers assume that an adult wrote the essays if there are two spaces after each sentence, as this used to be the rule. Now, most students are taught to use only one space after a sentence. Take note!

It is easy to spot the interloper when it comes to Soundbites as well. Don't get me wrong—parents can absolutely help their child with writing a Soundbite. In fact, I love hearing when an entire family does the Soundbite Exercise in order to learn together. Because the Soundbite concept can be done at any age from high school on, parents, older siblings, and grandparents can join in and discover something new about themselves. But in the end, the student needs to be driving both the college admissions process and the development of their Soundbite. When the student is not involved with writing their Soundbite or, worse yet, with working on their application, it is obvious.

A lot of times, the first version of a Soundbite that I review is written by a parent:

> Student designs, sews, and creates futuristic costumes and characters for the homemade movies he makes where he and his friends are the actors.

Not bad, right? Sounds pretty cool, actually. But it feels a little distant, like it was written for the student instead of the student writing it for himself. At the very least, he could make the all-important switch from the third person to the first person to get started. He could also make it his own:

I design, sew, and create futuristic costumes and characters for the sci-fi movies I shoot, edit, and star in with my friends.

Truth be told, this is my son. I hope he sees his talent the way I see it. If he does, he could write more than his own Soundbite. He could write his own ticket to Hollywood. However, ownership is fundamental in the Soundbite approach. Luckily we've got time on our side. He isn't in high school just yet.

Rule #1 puts the focus and onus on the student.

Shifting the language to the first person allows the student to embrace their Soundbite. It is the only way to protect the integrity of the process. When the Soundbite is written for the student instead of by the student, getting buy-in from them is challenging even if the Soundbite is highly effective. Once the student gets involved, the results can exceed their expectations.

The exercise for this rule is an easy one. Parents, if you are reading this book first, now is a great time to get your child to start reading it and have them take a stab at their own Soundbite or revise the one you wrote for them by shifting the pronouns to the first person.

It sounds so basic, but changing the Soundbite to the first person and having the student author it transforms the statement from something someone else believes about them into a reflection of the specialness they see in themselves. When that occurs, the Soundbite takes on a magical existence that is undeniable because it's the student's own words. That is a proud moment for all involved.

THIRD PERSON TO FIRST PERSON EXERCISE

Write out the current version of the Soundbite here:

_____

_____

_____

_____

1. Is the Soundbite written in the first person by the student? If so, you're ready for Rule #2. ☐ Yes ☐ No

2. If the Soundbite uses the third person, simply change the language to the first person here:

    _____

    _____

    _____

    _____

3. If the Soundbite is in the first person but was written by someone else, have the student write their own version in the first person here:

    _____

    _____

    _____

    _____

RULE #2: ONE CONCISE SENTENCE

Soundbites are a concentrated version of your application. The Soundbite is your "pitch." It does not need to be long or complex, as your actual college application has all the details anyone would need to know. In fact, succinctness is the goal in crafting your Soundbite because you don't know how much time you have to impress the recipient, and the application should have everything to back up your Soundbite and more.

And the same approach can be applied as an adult. Your Soundbite becomes your preparation before the phone call, the big job interview, the meeting with a book publisher (or TV producer, movie producer, etc.), or the appointment with investors about your business idea. The college application becomes the cover letter and résumé for the job, the proposal for the book, the business plan for your venture.

As I write this chapter in particular, I am reminded by a meeting I had with a literary agent when I was trying to secure a publisher for this book. When I learned that I got a meeting with this very powerful agent, I got fancied up and drove three hours from my home in Pennsylvania to New York City. I arrived thinking I was going to have at least an hour of one-on-one time with this literary legend, but instead I was brought back to the agent's "shared office." With two other junior agents staring at me while seemingly doing their own work, the agent asked me to describe my idea. I nervously started pouring out every last detail about my background and every job I'd had in the admissions field. I didn't even get to talk about my book before she gave me the "high sign" to conclude. Less than ten minutes after the meeting started, she showed me the door and told me to send my book proposal to her. As she said, if she wanted to know what my book was about, it would be in the proposal, right? Right. Boy, did I learn a valuable lesson that day.

You just don't know how much time you have with the individual on the receiving end. And while I am addressing the Soundbite concept right now, remember that the same thing goes for your application.

I wouldn't say less is more when it comes to the application. Rather, use the application to its fullest when it comes to the required sections. Use every character you can in the activities section. Use every word before reaching the word count to write the most fully developed essays. And answer every question about race, language, and religion to make sure that AOs aren't misrepresenting you. Remember that the Soundbite approach allows you to give them the most accurate and powerful sense of who you are. Make sure your Soundbite inspires you to do this as you fill out applications. But not only is submitting extra materials in the application unnecessary—it is often unwanted.

Extra words in the Soundbite make it cumbersome and hard to remember. Extra materials in the application that are not required make it similarly cumbersome. In fact, the only thing that a student is remembered for in this situation is the fact that he overloaded his application with pieces that were not explicitly asked for. Those unnecessary pieces often come in the form of the following: résumé, using the additional information section unnecessarily, a research paper, extra letters of recommendation, extra essays that were not requested, and extensive emails from the student or about the student from parents and school officials (yes, these often make it into the application too).

But I digress. Back to the Soundbite! Use your words thoughtfully in the Soundbite. Think about it. If the person on the receiving end is curious and wants more detail, they will give you verbal and nonverbal cues to keep going and explain yourself. But they can also rely on the application as long as your Soundbite has guided you through it. Your Soundbite should be concise and powerful. Long-windedness is not your friend when it comes to setting yourself apart in any setting, environment, or industry.

Starting with a concise and powerful message about yourself can pique the interest of the person on the receiving end. If they are so intrigued, they will be willing to invest more time in learning more about you in your application.

Rule #2: One sentence is all you get for your Soundbite! It will force you to pack a lot of punch in a short amount of space.

Most of my students have trouble condensing their specialness into just one sentence, though. I feel their pain! If given the floor, I have always been able to start talking without a care in the world, especially when I was younger. Yet self-awareness (remember that trait from Part 1?) today keeps me in check.

Conciseness doesn't limit the message; it allows you to gauge the recipient's reaction and how much time you have to explain yourself further and forces you to focus on quality interactions with individuals and organizations who value you.

That literary agent did not want to represent me. But I had learned my lesson. My second pitch with a literary agent was a lot more successful because my message was clear and not bogged down with unnecessary information. And when it came time to pitch my book proposal to publishers, my Soundbite was clear—literally and figuratively. But it took time to hone the message even though I had a lot of practice beforehand. Just like your craft, the Soundbite is something to constantly work on and improve for conciseness and effectiveness.

What often happens with that first pitch, first draft of a college essay, or first stab at a Soundbite is that you're onto something special, but it is just so long or convoluted that the specialness gets lost in all the words. Take, for example, the following Soundbite, which was written as a first attempt by an Application Nation student after doing the Soundbite Exercise:

I am a builder of communities, of dreams, of robots, of spirit, of minds and of computer code, having conceptualized and created a coalition of robotics teams that now includes over 250 teams from nineteen countries, having been state dean's list semifinalist as the lead designer and a software engineer on my high school's robotics team who won the regional Inspire Award and State of Indiana Control Award for programming, leading my state's chapter of a Ukraine-based community of FIRST robotics students to raise awareness for environmental policies in engineering, organizing and leading a project during the COVID-19 pandemic to produce PPE for first responders which has produced nearly one thousand face shields, designing robots to help package COVID-19 vaccines, leading the way to create a makerspace at my high school, serving as a founding member of my school's GirlsCode chapter, bringing positive energy to multiple communities having won Spirit Awards from my school's marching band three years running, my overnight camp as the single senior camper to win their Spirit Award, also bringing my spirit to my school and club water polo, swim teams, and school tutoring network through motivation and work ethic in and out of the pool.

Earnest as anyone, this student tried to follow my rules by making the Soundbite one sentence long. But that's one long sentence! Impressive, though!

Granted, the Soundbite is not listed in the application, and it doesn't need to pass a grammar test. But you don't need to put everything special about yourself into it. You just want to string together the highlights in a thematic way.

So I challenge my students to take out unnecessary words in the Soundbite that any student could use to describe themselves. I also encourage them to avoid being too list-y. That's what the activities and honors section of the application is for. The goal of the Soundbite is to capture specialness in a concise way so that the power of the student's statement clarifies their identity, guides their application process, and piques the recipient's interest.

For my student who wrote a powerful yet longer Soundbite the first time around, I wanted to assure her that all of that good stuff (or almost all of it) would be captured in her application. I wanted her Soundbite to be shorter, yet concentrated enough to deliver just as much punch. This was the final version we came up with:

> I use technology to build and strengthen communities, creating over 250 robotics teams in nineteen countries, producing one thousand face shields, designing robots to help package COVID-19 vaccines, and raising awareness of environmental policies in engineering.

This student's original Soundbite was 201 words; the revised Soundbite is 36. It does not include everything she has done or is currently doing, but that's not the point. It should hint at everything she plans to include in her application.

From this student's revised Soundbite, it is obvious what she does in her spare time and suggests what she wants to pursue academically in college. The Soundbite gives us a window into not only how productive she is but how far her reach is.

I should add that this young woman's main college essay had nothing to do with engineering or robots. As I often say, that is perfect information for a college's more specific supplemental essays. Instead, the topic she chose to write about for her main essay spoke to her mature perspective and generous spirit, which comes through in her Soundbite. She ended up writing about how her high school gymnasium, the place that had held so many wonderful memories for her growing up, turned in high school into an environment of bullying, of which she was the target. In the end, she became a leader in her high school instead of a victim and realized the power of her "reach" when she did.

When I am reviewing a student's application before they submit it to a college, I write my own Soundbite on the student as if I were still an AO. It helps me confirm that the student's Soundbite comes through so beautifully and powerfully that even a stranger (which most AOs are to students) could come away with both a complimentary and a complementary Soundbite on the student. Here is my AO version of this student's application:

> This young woman will make a remarkable engineer someday as she has all the academic and extracurricular pieces of evidence to support it, but she already is a remarkable human being, and there is no other student I would want on our campus more than her—ADMIT.

Students don't have access to what the actual AO wrote after reading their application. Even with the Family Educational Rights and Privacy Act, subjective critiques like an AO's Soundbite or summary are usually expunged before students enroll and have the ability to look at what's left of their application. However, every AO has to write a version of a Soundbite. It is the only way to prove they fully read the application and have a statement to back up the admissions decision. We want the AO's Soundbite to be as accurate and reminiscent of the student's own Soundbite. If the student uses their Soundbite as their conscience, their application will support it, thus allowing the AO to come away with a similar message about the student. But keeping it concise and making sure every word counts helps the student focus on what truly sets them apart.

For many of us, we want to prove ourselves. We equate quantity with success. More is not better when it comes to the Soundbite or pitch. It is not about throwing in every possible detail; it is about picking the right words to show boldness, distinctiveness, and positivity about ourselves in a concise, deliberate way.

And the longer you subscribe to the Soundbite approach, the more you can tweak, hone, and often shorten your Soundbite. Remember my longer version before I had a stake in the industry? It is thirty-six words:

> I am America's College Counselor, providing high-quality college admissions advice to all families through monthly Facebook Lives, a weekly blog, and up-to-the-hour responses to the thousands of members of the online community I built, Application Nation.

Yet five words can do wonders for piquing someone's interest:

I am America's College Counselor.

Bold, distinctive, positive, concise. I can easily provide more details once I make this statement, and I know the recipient is open to hearing more from me. But being this succinct has opened up doors I never knew I had access to. They gave me the opportunity to not only write a book but get it published.

These five words also keep me honest. If I get distracted by other things or people, it doesn't take me long to get back on track. If I am truly America's College Counselor, I should be working on that statement every single day of my life (or close to it).

Your one-sentence Soundbite doesn't have to be five words like my abbreviated version, but it should be a sentence that isn't a mouthful. Whether you are working on your application or describing yourself to someone, you want your Soundbite to guide you, inspire you, and keep you focused on what matters. When that happens, the admissions officer has a very clear visual of you.

The exercise for this rule is straightforward. It is about making sure your Soundbite is one concise sentence, without taking away the boldness, distinctiveness, and positivity of what you are trying to say. While some sentences have more words than others, grammar experts often say that a sentence should have fifteen to twenty words. That can be hard to do for a student. So if we double that, the student's Soundbite can be up to forty words.

Let's get to work and try to get that Soundbite down to forty words or fewer!

POWER OF THE PITHY PITCH EXERCISE

Step 1: Write down your current Soundbite below:

_____

_____

_____

Step 2: Is it one sentence? If not, make it one sentence here:

_____

_____

_____

Step 3: An ideal sentence is fifteen to twenty words long! Your Soundbite doesn't have to be this short. Double the limit if necessary, which means forty words should be the maximum. Rewrite your Soundbite below in forty words or fewer. It takes some practice to do this and some letting go as well! Write down Soundbite 2.0 here:

_____

_____

_____

Step 4: If you are having trouble meeting this word count or you feel like you want to take it to the next level (and of course you do!), read on.

Rule #2 is all about the one-sentence Soundbite. The power of the pithy pitch is everything!

RULE #3: PRESENT TENSE

One of the first things I teach families with younger students about getting into college is that the process is focused on high school. Some ask, "Well what about middle school achievements?" I kindly respond by explaining that AOs are interested almost exclusively in the ninth through twelfth grades. That means that AOs at most colleges don't spend time on whether a middle school student took a high school class, although many students do, and many high school transcripts even include them. And there isn't even an option for the student to list activities or honors before ninth grade on the application.

It is what is taken, done, and achieved *in* high school that matters to colleges. It can be a harsh reality, especially for a student who experienced great success in middle school. However, the process encourages all of us to not live in the past. It holds students accountable for who they are now and how they spend their four years of high school.

Below is an example of a student's Soundbite that focuses on middle school accomplishments rather than high school. It is a reminder that they aren't applying for high school admission; they are applying to get into college.

> I won the national spelling bee when I was in seventh grade.

This is what I call a "Soundbite of the Past." This example can be applied to a student who achieved similar success as an athlete, actor, writer, or other type of standout in middle school or even earlier. The student is so focused on this achievement and letting everyone know about it that it dominates his application: all of his letter writers mention this in their recommendation letters, sometimes the student writes one of their essays about it, and/or they provide additional information (that is not asked for) about this achievement. As a result, the AO comes away knowing a lot about who this student *was* but very little about who this student *is* five years later. Below is a Soundbite written by an AO after reading this type of application:

> Impressive that this student won the national spelling bee in seventh grade, but he seems to rely on that instead of using it as inspiration for doing something meaningful in high school—DENY.

However, if that student used this achievement from seventh grade as the first step rather than the last step, the student, their Soundbite, and their application can take on greater meaning. For example, strong spelling and grammar skills can lead the student to join their school's newspaper in ninth grade as a writer and to become the editor in chief by senior year. Alternatively, the student could build a platform where the spelling bee competition could grow nationally from just a middle school event to one for high school students too. While the spelling bee achievement from seventh grade should not be mentioned in the Soundbite, it can surely serve as a foundation for what is to come. Look at how his Soundbite could evolve:

> I am the creator of the national spelling bee competition for high school students, growing this annual event from just seventh and eighth graders to ninth through twelfth graders, making spelling a passion for all.

Living in the past slows you down and doesn't allow you to grow and evolve. Living in the present is the most powerful vehicle to personal achievement and making the greatest impact on our world.

This approach about not living in the past has staying power even into adulthood. One of my students was interviewed on campus by an AO. The interviewer not only dominated the conversation but kept repeating that he used to be an investment banker on Wall Street. My student was so turned off by his seeming attachment to his past glory that she no longer wanted to apply there. It helped her to realize that someone's harping on the past gets tiresome for the person on the receiving end. Living in the present gives us urgency and deliberateness.

Many of us have experienced this on both ends. I have been on the receiving end of many students who have defined themselves by something in their past. I have been guilty of doing the same thing. For a few years after I left my job as a dean of admissions, I defined myself by the past when I met someone new. I would often share, "I used to be the dean of admissions at Franklin & Marshall College." Most people were kind to my face. But I cringe reliving this. If I were on the receiving end of this Soundbite of the Past, I would think that this person was embarrassed about what they were currently doing or simply not embracing their current self. When I shifted my mindset from the past to the present and started making the most of each day, my career took off and carried me much further than that dean of admissions job, by the way!

Similarly, focusing on the future has just as many pitfalls as living in the past. Take a look at this common student Soundbite as an example:

I want to be a doctor.

Yes, this is written in the first person, and it sure is concise. Rules #1 and #2 are satisfied. However, instead of focusing on what he actively does that is related to medicine, the student focuses on his dream for the future. As much as I love ambitious students, I encourage them to focus less on the end goal and more on the here and now. In other words, if a student wants to become a doctor, what classes and standardized tests should he be taking, what activities should he be doing, and what personal traits is he developing right now to reach this goal? When a student pays so much attention to a future goal, he misses out on what's going on right in front of him. The AO responds like this:

> Just another student who wants to be a doctor—DENY.

There is nothing wrong with having professional, educational, or personal goals for the future, but the Soundbite concept forces us to do everything we can right now to reach those goals. That's the difference.

Yet, one of the hardest parts of working with ambitious students is getting them to realize that their Soundbite doesn't have to match up exactly to their future goals. I remember meeting one of my former students for the first time. It was clear from her transcript and a few minutes of conversation that she wanted to be premed in college and ultimately wanted to become a physician. She had the classes and grades to back that up, but so do a lot of students. She could have easily had the above-mentioned Soundbite, but we worked hard to make sure she didn't.

One of the most impressive things about this student was something she was doing well before she met me. It was related to science and medicine, but not in the traditional sense. She demonstrated her commitment to the field through advocacy work related to the antivaping laws in her home state. Take a look at her Soundbite:

> I am the brains and courage behind my state's antivaping campaign, which teaches teens my mantra: do the right thing instead of the popular thing. (Stanford University)

Sometimes, though, a student doesn't have the experience they want just yet. It doesn't just happen with younger students; it can happen with anyone who has a dream and just needs focus and direction to make it happen. This is when the "Aspirational Soundbite" comes in handy with students who need a little help. I use it sparingly—only if I have to.

The Aspirational Soundbite follows Rule #1 of being written in the first person and Rule #2 of being one concise sentence. And it technically follows Rule #3 as it is written in the present tense. But it is what I hope the student will start doing very soon rather than what they are actually doing right now.

For example, students often have goals in mind but don't have the evidence to create a final Soundbite:

- The student who wants to go to film school but hasn't made a film yet
- The student who wants to major in business but doesn't know why because they haven't done anything related to business just yet
- The student who wants to major in politics but doesn't have any experience

- The student who tells me they want to be a forensics expert because they love the *CSI* television show

I don't doubt these students' aspirations, but AOs are looking for evidence that can be quantified and backed up in the application. These students can still put together an Aspirational Soundbite. In fact, all Soundbites, whether written or imagined, begin as an aspirational idea. The Aspirational Soundbite can turn into a real, authentic Soundbite as long as the student follows through with their intentions.

The future film student:

> I write, direct, and star in my own films (in and around my hometown) about teenagers facing life's complicated issues of love, loss, and following your dreams.

The future business student:

> I research and analyze how successful companies survive during economic downturns to help our family-owned business stay afloat during the 2020 recession.

The future politician:

> I started as a campaign volunteer going door-to-door, but it has turned into my becoming the youngest staffer for the future congresswoman from my district!

The forensics student:

> When the county medical examiner taught an introductory class on forensics at my school, I took it, and it landed me an internship with him observing autopsies and helping him prepare medical reports.

Intrinsic to the Soundbite concept is being resourceful. Oftentimes students think they need to spend a lot of money to have the most extraordinary Soundbite. But what allows an ordinary student to have an extraordinary Soundbite is doing a lot with very little. Expensive summer programs may give a student structure and a forced environment to create something, but it's not the same as doing it from scratch on your own. And fancy internships with VIPs are often looked at with disdain as they suggest family connections and privilege more than initiative.

The only thing that an aspiring film student needs is motivation and a camera. The business student needs to look within herself and realize that opportunities to get hands-on experience are right in front of her. The politics lover needs to roll up his sleeves, literally go door-to-door, and have doors slammed in his face to know what it's really like to work in the industry. The *CSI* aficionado needs to get off her couch to ensure the smell of formaldehyde doesn't make her faint before committing to forensics.

In the end, I like to give a student time to get moving on an Aspirational Soundbite. If nothing happens in the first month, it usually isn't going to happen, at which point the student needs to pivot and find something more realistic and authentic to who they are. Aspirational Soundbites are just temporary. They need to turn into one concise sentence, written in the first person and in the present tense, and be accurate and truthful to have a transformational effect on the student and anyone on the receiving end.

The exercise for Rule #3 is an easy fix on the Soundbite as long as you are living by it. For those students working off an Aspirational Soundbite, make sure it embodies evidence you can attain now rather than years down the road.

Rule #3 is all about living in the present and seizing the moment.

LIVE IN THE PRESENT EXERCISE

1. List your current Soundbite here:

    _____

    _____

    _____

    _____

2. Are there any past- or future-tense verbs or phrases? If so, rewrite your
    Soundbite by removing and replacing them with present-tense verbs and
    current experiences below.　☐ Yes ☐ No

    _____

    _____

    _____

    _____

3. If you are having trouble switching to the present tense due to the fact that
    your Soundbite is aspirational, list what you want to do to back it up using
    present tense verbs and give yourself one month to get things moving:

    _____

    _____

    _____

    _____

RULE #4: USE NOUNS AND VERBS, NOT ADJECTIVES

You can't surprise me. I've seen every possible adjective written about students hundreds, even thousands of times. It does not matter how unusual the adjective is; it has been used by a student to describe him- or herself or by a teacher or counselor to describe a student. I am immune to them at this point. In fact, I grimace a bit every time I see one. The fact is that adjectives can be used again and again for many students. And anything that is done that many times in the admissions process means that the AO won't be moved by it. AOs like to be surprised and hear novel things about a student.

The college process makes it hard to avoid these overused and replaceable adjectives, though. One of the most popular questions on a "brag sheet" (a form that students or parents fill out before a counselor of record or teacher writes the student's letter) is the following: "List three, four, or five adjectives to describe yourself." That's when I find myself saying in slow motion, "Nooooooooooo!" The counselor or teacher often uses these adjectives verbatim in the letter of recommendation they write for the student. When I see adjectives in a letter of recommendation, I know it's a missed opportunity. The teacher or counselor uses adjectives as a crutch instead of writing about their own impressions of the student. I am not a fan of crutches when we are talking about real people. Adjectives are a time-saving approach for letter writers, but they serve very few students well.

Listing adjectives is also a common approach to a popular essay prompt like Stanford's former request "What five words best describe you." Almost every single time, the student responds with five adjectives. Noooooooo. Stanford wasn't asking for adjectives per se. So be creative. Be bold. Not just for Stanford, but in describing yourself to others!

Nouns and verbs are much more powerful than adjectives. It is much less common for students to repeat nouns and verbs that other students have used before. There are nearly twenty-three thousand nouns and verbs compared to only ten thousand adjectives in the English language. I know what parts of speech I would choose for my Soundbite and any form that allows me to describe myself.

Take a look at a Soundbite from a former student of mine:

> I am **responsible** and **hardworking**, and I see opportunity in everything to help others.

Responsible. Hardworking. Helps others.

These are all really positive ways to describe a student or yourself, but they are some of the most common ways as well. If I didn't know how special this student was, I would believe she was indistinguishable from everyone else. I have read so many applications that just blend in because the students don't see themselves as influencers (in the traditional sense rather than the social media sense) or in action; they see themselves as modifiers. That's what adjectives are. They can't stand on their own. And when that happens, the AO writes a Soundbite like this:

> A nice young woman who is responsible, hardworking, and helps others, but nothing stands out—DENY.

Fortunately, this student's Soundbite didn't end there. We tweaked her Soundbite, activities list, messaging to her letter writers, and essays to embody this version:

> I am both a humanitarian and fashion designer for people in need from my home state and a voice for their concerns in public government and student government on the local, state, and national levels.

The AO surely came away with something similarly profound as this:

> High-achieving student who has done more for the people of her home state than any politician—watch out world, this young woman is the ultimate contributor to society—ADMIT!

Again, there is no way of knowing what an AO's Soundbite looks like, but you want them to see in you what you see in yourself. When moved by a student, an AO will go to bat for them with a Soundbite that moves an entire admissions committee. This student enrolled at Brown University.

Here's another example from a former student of mine. Below is his first version of his Soundbite. As you can tell, the first draft was not written in the first person. But focus on the adjectives and adverbs in it:

Original Soundbite:

> **Extremely bright, outgoing young** man who is **passionate** about building relationships, providing **exceptional** customer service, and ensuring **excellent** guest experiences.

This is very positive, but I can't visualize who this young man is beyond a bunch of modifiers. He had such a great story to back up these adjectives and adverbs. Here is his revised Soundbite written in the first person with nouns and verbs:

> I belong in the field of hospitality, and I have taken every class I can and spend my free time working in the industry to know this—I even show up at the restaurant on my day off.

And the AO's version of his Soundbite:

> If you own a restaurant or business, this is who you hire because he's the only employee who shows up on his day off and leaps into action like a superhero the moment he sees a need—ADMIT.

The reference to showing up at the restaurant in the student's and AO's Soundbites is a hint at what came through in the rest of his application. It serves as an activator in his Soundbite where we can visualize who this special young man is.

Removing adjectives and adverbs transforms a Soundbite and forces the student to get specific about who they are in their public and private worlds. This student references going to the restaurant where he worked on his day off, but it doesn't describe exactly what happened when he arrived. That's okay. His application filled in the blanks and described him literally leaping into action to help a customer in need on his day off. The CEO of the company heard about his good deed and wrote a letter to thank him. His counselor of record got a copy of the letter—not necessarily to send along to colleges, as "extra materials" are not always welcomed. But the counselor referenced the CEO's gratitude in the formal letter of recommendation submitted on behalf of the student.

Remember that the Soundbite doesn't have to include everything in it. It's almost like a teaser to what is actually in the application. This student's Soundbite paid off. He went to the Dedman School of Hospitality at Florida State University.

One of the hardest things about writing (and living) an original and moving Soundbite is avoiding adjectives and adverbs and using nouns and verbs instead. It is almost as hard as writing your first Soundbite because it challenges the student to think much deeper about himself. He cannot rely on safe go-to words, like modifiers. He must view himself as an activator. Modifiers rely on other people and things. Activators are bold enough to go out on a limb and do what no one else is doing. They aren't afraid to be different.

Everyone has the power to be an activator. It is all about how you see yourself and how you project yourself.

Rule #4 is about using nouns and verbs in the Soundbite rather than relying on replaceable and unremarkable adjectives and adverbs.

MODIFIER VERSUS ACTIVATOR EXERCISE

1. Take your Soundbite 3.0 and list it below. Circle all adjectives and adverbs. Everything circled must go or be replaced with nouns and verbs.

    _____

    _____

    _____

    _____

2. Write your Soundbite 4.0 full of nouns and verbs below:

    _____

    _____

    _____

    _____

RULE #5: NO ONE ELSE IN THE WORLD CAN HAVE YOUR SOUNDBITE

The only way to stand out in the admissions process and in life is to do things differently—and be willing to share this. Once you dip your toes into following your heart and activating something within you, your confidence grows exponentially.

It takes guts, though. There will be plenty of doubters along the way. There may even be some bullies too. But if anyone makes fun of you about how you are living your Soundbite, that's a sign to keep doing it. Those who tease or bully feel less fulfilled by what they are doing. Their insecurity comes through when they see someone (that's you!) living the life they wish they themselves had the confidence to live.

But before you feel like this process only rewards those who do something monumental as a teenager, like discovering an unknown math theory or creating a social justice movement from scratch, consider what you currently do and how you approach the pursuit or delivery differently than everyone around you.

Most high school students do similar types of activities—sports, performing arts, clubs, service work, or part-time jobs. There is nothing wrong with wanting to feel like a typical teenager and doing activities like this. But I encourage students who are doing the more common activities to do things in an uncommon way.

For example, many students are members of their high school's junior varsity or varsity sports teams. They might not get recruited to play collegiate sports. Heck, many of them may not make it to varsity or see playing time in high school. One could see that as a limitation, but I see it as an opportunity to do something uncommon.

What if you played a different role on your high school sports team besides the star varsity athlete? It could be as simple as making energy bars for game day. Those energy bars could turn into something much bigger than just fuel for your teammates, especially if they taste good and give everyone a sustaining jolt of energy when they need it. The sky's the limit when you take a risk and do something that no one else is doing. Who knows, those energy bars could end up being sold in stores before you even apply to college.

But even if your energy bar only gets eaten by your teammates, there is a way to translate this selfless act into a Soundbite that ultimately guides everything from a student's intended major, to how she describes her role on the team on her activities list, to the teachers who write her letters of recommendation, to the topics she chooses to write about for her essays.

Let's see this play out. If this student's Soundbite is as follows, look at how she transforms from just another student athlete who may even "sit the bench" for all four years of high school into an individual with a distinctive Soundbite doing things that no one else around her is doing:

Student's Soundbite:

> I study the intersection between neuroscience and nutrition, which leads me to make energy bars for my team on game days, as I discovered that even those players who sit the bench (including me!) need a jolt of serotonin.

Student's intended major/minor:

> Neuroscience major with a minor in nutrition

Sample activity listing on the Common Application that meets the strict character count:

Role (50-character max):

> Official Energy Bar Baker and Player

Organization (100-character max):

> East High School Girls' Field Hockey Team

Description (150-character max):

> Discovered my love for baking on the field hockey team when I saw that players (starters and bench warmers) needed a serotonin boost before games.

Recommendation letter choice:

> Junior year AP Biology teacher who not only taught me in a core academic class but also serves as my unofficial mentor for the independent research I do on neuroscience and nutrition.

Supplemental essay topic on student's academic interest:

> How the current research I am conducting on depression and athletes can be addressed through increasing serotonin from tryptophan in energy bars I make from scratch.

Even if this student's research is simply self-guided without publication or formal lab work, the message is clear: she is actively pursuing her interest on a daily basis and turning something common, like playing a sport, into something uncommon and extraordinary. I call this intersection or confluence of interests the "special-special," and Chapter 13 is devoted entirely to this concept. The special-special brings together different fields of study or interests and allows the student to carve out a niche for him- or herself. The result is an AO's Soundbite like this:

> This student has taken her role as bench warmer on the field hockey team to become a budding nutritional neuroscientist who fuels her mind and her teammates with homemade energy bars to boost serotonin—ADMIT!

Sometimes the student has to shift their role or pivot to craft the most distinctive Soundbite. Many times, though, they are already doing something different, but they don't recognize it or are not projecting that to others.

One of my former students wrote the following Soundbite:

> A **true** leader with a sense of social responsibility and **intellectual** curiosity who is making an impact on her community.

I know what you're thinking!

Rule #1: It is not written in the first person.

Rule #2: It's definitely one concise sentence, though. Only twenty words!

Rule #3: Verbs are present tense. Yay!

Rule #4: Adjectives are being used. And some of the nouns and phrases are very common and overused buzzwords in college admissions: "leader," "social responsibility," "curiosity," "impact on [the] community." Even though there are some nouns and verbs here, the Soundbite feels generic, right?

To fulfill Rule #5, this student needed a Soundbite that no one else in the world had. So we took another stab at it to meet all of the rules. Notice in her revised Soundbite how she introduces her family's unusual background. That is totally fair game for the Soundbite. And while her "community" means so much to her, she never uses that common buzzword.

> I am the daughter of refugees in a town that has welcomed us, and I am compelled to show my gratitude through my work as an EMT and active participant in our local government.

This student listed political science and public policy as her intended majors but also made clear she wanted to pursue the premed track in her application. While being premed is very common these days, she turned her academic interests into something more specific. Here's how an AO would sum her up in a Soundbite:

> This young woman walks the walk when it comes to making a connection between public health and community engagement, and her own hometown is the beneficiary of an unusually generous teenager ready to do even greater things in college and beyond—ADMIT.

This student proudly attends Washington University.

And if you need another example to prove that you don't have to do something new to make your Soundbite distinct, here is a story about one of my favorite students to wrap up this chapter.

As I often say, it's never too early or too late to write your Soundbite. This particular student didn't start working with me until days before his senior year of high school. In that first meeting, he declared that he was interested in public health with a possible interest in medicine down the road. He presented himself as passionate (yep, there's one of those buzzwords again) about community service (and another buzzword) and diversity (and yet another buzzword). Some may think that being a majority student working within the diversity space was his ticket into the elite colleges on his list. As much as what he was doing at his school was incredibly impressive, there were other students (even classmates of his) doing the same exact thing. I never asked him for a Soundbite 1.0, but my guess is that it would have been dominated by buzzwords like "passionate," "community service," and "diversity." It didn't matter that his grades and scores would make him "competitive" at any college. His Soundbite, and thus his application, wouldn't help him stand out in a highly competitive applicant pool.

He could have started something new in senior year, as plenty of students find their footing during their last year of high school. But he wouldn't have as much time to develop it, at least not for his college applications. Instead, I pointed out to him what piqued my interest as a former AO: the highly unusual high school class on his transcript from junior year, titled "Botany." I asked him about it, and he replied that he was intrigued to take the class after working at his high school's greenhouse.

Greenhouse? Wait just one second.

Greenhouse? Yes, that's right.

And it turned out that he would be in charge of the greenhouse for senior year and would be taking AP Environmental Science too. And, by the way, he had just started doing fieldwork with his state's Department of Agriculture on indigenous plants.

I asked him if he had ever considered majoring in environmental science. I explained that he could go to medical school with any major he wanted. In fact, as with the admissions process for college, doing things differently helps you stand out in the admissions process for med school too. After a few weeks, during which I wondered if I had scared him off, he came back with energy and passion. He was ready to embrace this Soundbite:

> I am a cultivator of plants and relationships, and I see my world as a greenhouse, ensuring that those in my care and company feel the warmth of the human spirit.

We spent the next few weeks and months making sure his Soundbite resonated in his application. It wasn't about hammering the environmental piece home in every section of the application. Every activity he did wasn't about environmental work. Instead it was about layering the tenets of his Soundbite throughout the application.

We made some deliberate choices once the Soundbite was written. He checked the environmental science major on all of his applications. We re-ordered the activities list a bit: the greenhouse job had been buried at the bottom despite the number of hours he devoted to it and the leadership role he had been given. And we added the new role at the Department of Agriculture to the list, detailing exactly what he was doing there in the field.

While his main essay had nothing to do with his newly appreciated academic interest (and it never should), it was a chance to highlight how important relationships and the human spirit were to him. In other words, his main essay evoked his Soundbite without ever using any of the terminology.

The ultimate expression of his Soundbite came through in a supplemental essay about how some obscure class like "Botany" could lead to such a revelation about his number one academic pursuit at that moment. Almost every elite college will require a supplemental essay of varying length devoted to the student's main academic interest.

This is why I tell students never to write about their academic interest in their main essay if they are applying to highly selective colleges, since they will have to write about it for most of the supplemental essays required. Hammering or repeating one theme in every section of the application doesn't work; layering does. It's not about overwhelming the application with one theme; it's about layering and showing how the Soundbite serves as inspiration or fuel for how the student lives their life.

After reading his powerful application, an AO could write a Soundbite like this:

He is a force of nature, and nature has never seen someone so engaged in the environment, people, and societal issues on our planet—ADMIT!

Again, we will never see an AO's actual Soundbite since notes like this are so influential in the admissions process that they are typically expunged by the admissions office at the end of the cycle. Yet, based on my careful review of his application, I believe an AO would make a similarly moving statement. This young man enrolled at the University of North Carolina at Chapel Hill.

That's the power of a Soundbite. That's the power of being self-aware about your strengths and limitations, being intentional about choices, and being willing to tell your story, which is far different from those of everyone around you.

Rule #5 ensures that no one else in the world could string together the Soundbite you have written. Only you can.

The final exercise for Part 2 is tweaking your Soundbite to fulfill Rule #5. This will make it a statement that no one else in the world could say about him- or herself. It is quite empowering, so let's get to it.

TRULY DISTINCTIVE SOUNDBITE EXERCISE

List your current Soundbite here:

_____

_____

_____

_____

Step 1: Does it fulfill Rule #1? Is it written in the first person? ☐ Yes ☐ No

Step 2: Does it fulfill Rule #2? Is it a one-sentence Soundbite of forty words or fewer? ☐ Yes ☐ No

Step 3: Does it fulfill Rule #3? Is it written in the present tense to reflect who you are right now? ☐ Yes ☐ No

Step 4: Does it fulfill Rule #4? Did you remove extra adjectives and adverbs (and even common buzzwords) and replace them with bold nouns and verbs? ☐ Yes ☐ No

Step 5: Does it fulfill Rule #5? Are you the only person in the world (or around you) who could have written this Soundbite? ☐ Yes ☐ No

Step 6: If you answered yes to all the previous questions, you have your Soundbite.

Step 7: If you answered no to anything, specifically Rule #5, this is your chance to make your Soundbite so authentic that no one else could say it about him- or herself.

I encourage anyone struggling to meet these rules to simply make a list of nouns and verbs that could be truly distinctive to them individually or strung together in a sentence.

Here are five nouns that describe one of my Application Nation students:

1. American Samoan
2. Harpist
3. Chemistry
4. Material science
5. Cultural identity

Look how he can string them together and create a Soundbite that fulfills all the rules and says something that no one else in the world could say about him- or herself:

> I am an American Samoan harpist who is interested in chemistry, specifically material science, because I like to study not only what things are made up of but also what makes up each individual's cultural identity.

The words you list can form the foundation of or, at the very least, serve as inspiration for your Soundbite.

SOUNDBITE 5.0 EXERCISE

If you are struggling, list five nouns or verbs that represent you here:

_____

_____

_____

_____

1. Take another stab at your Soundbite, keeping in mind the five rules: (1) written in the first person, (2) one concise sentence (forty words max), (3) written in the present tense, (4) using nouns and verbs, and (5) a true statement about yourself that no one else could say but you. List your new Soundbite here:

    _____

    _____

    _____

    _____

2. If your Soundbite is more aspirational right now, what classes, activities, and experiences can you pursue starting today to make it more of a reality?

    _____

    _____

    _____

3. Look at your nouns and verbs from question #1. Does your Soundbite resonate with your choices? ☐ Yes ☐ No

4. Are you the only one who could say this about yourself? If yes, you've got
   your Soundbite. If no, what could you add or replace that will make it one
   of a kind?   ☐ Yes ☐ No

   _____

   _____

   _____

   _____

PART 3

LIVING YOUR

S⊚UNDBITE

CHAPTER 11

The College List

It is one thing to say your Soundbite out loud or even write it out, but it's only true and authentic if you live by it. This takes commitment and an ability to avoid distractions—peers, doubters, and the expectations of others. If a student is truly self-aware and intentional and is the ultimate storyteller of their life, Part 3 will inspire them to drive this process and be thoughtful about the decisions they make, including the colleges they choose to put on their list.

The most mature and self-aware students are able to put together a list of colleges that will value their strengths instead of those that will hyperanalyze their limitations. Yet the college list can start sooner than one might think. Having a Soundbite in place even as early as ninth grade can be helpful to students in determining what is important to them *at that moment*, knowing full well that the Soundbite can and should evolve over time.

While most high school students don't have a "final list" of colleges until senior year, they can have a "starter list" during their freshman and sophomore years and an "intermediate list" during junior year in order to get a feel for what they want and what will be required for admission and to complete all or most of their visits (virtual or in person) before senior year begins.

Most starter lists are short, usually containing a handful of colleges that the student has heard of or dreamed about but hasn't done a lot of research on. And oftentimes, the starter list includes only "reach" colleges to which admission is very competitive.

But as the student begins to visit or investigate these starter colleges, she must include colleges that are more realistic or have higher acceptance rates. No matter how competitive a student is, I always recommend "target" and "likely" schools. This is how the intermediate list begins to evolve and grow. In fact, the intermediate list is usually twice or three times as long as the starter list.

But the final list, which is often not "final" until the start of senior year, should not be too long or too short. I generally recommend a final college list ranging from nine to twelve colleges with at least an equal number of reach, target, and likely schools on it. Students with more limitations, like lower grades, for example, should have more target and likely schools than reach schools to ensure that they have as many choices at the end of the process as possible.

With students applying to more colleges than they did in previous generations and the fact that a majority of colleges factor "demonstrated interest" into the admissions process, getting started on some visits earlier in high school is sometimes the only way to ensure the final college list is a sound one.

It is so easy to be swayed by rankings, reputations, and even family members when it comes to the college list. But the point of applying to college is to *get into college*! Students need to have colleges on their list that not only appreciate them but will admit them. I like to review each of my students' list several times during high school to ensure each school is a match (both academically and personally) and resonates with their Soundbite. One of the most heartbreaking scenarios is when a family reaches out to me for the first time upon their child not getting admitted anywhere or only getting into colleges they are not interested in attending. This can occur when the student doesn't apply to colleges that value who they are and what they can offer.

To get you started, review my definitions of reach, target, and likely colleges for high-achieving students below. As you can see, these designations have little to do with a student's own qualifications, especially with a starter or intermediate college list. Part of that has to do with the fact that ninth and tenth graders typically haven't taken any official standardized tests. The other piece of it is that having the objective criteria (grades, curriculum, test scores) is no longer a guarantee of getting into certain colleges. Objective criteria can ensure the student is "competitive" for the college, but oftentimes the decision comes down to the subjective pieces of the application in the end.

> *Reach colleges:* I consider any college with an acceptance rate of 25 percent or less to be a "reach" no matter who the student is. Being aware of a college's acceptance rate when building the college list allows the student to acknowledge that it is less about their own limitations in this process and more about the college's.
>
> *Target colleges:* Colleges with overall acceptance rates of 26 to 50 percent are considered "targets" for most high achievers. While a 50 percent admit rate seems generous, most colleges will have a shockingly low acceptance rate in the Regular Decision round (which is when most students apply) due to an aggressive "early"

round. We can't take too many chances in formulating a college list. If the student applies to a target college during Early Decision, their chances of admission will go up. But if they apply during Regular Decision, that target college may look like a reach college due to the later deadline. And most of the time, colleges won't provide their acceptance rates for different programs like Early Decision and Regular Decision. Instead, you can only access their overall acceptance rate, so be cautious about it!

Likely colleges: If a college's acceptance rate is above 50 percent, most students (as long as they have strong/solid grades, curricula, and scores) will "likely" get admitted. Notice that I didn't say "will get admitted." Because many private colleges use demonstrated interest and public/state universities give preference to in-state applicants, it is hard to predict decisions. However, a college with an acceptance rate above 50 percent is usually a good likely school for most high-achieving students.

While acceptance rates drive my perspective, it is essential that a student's actual test scores, curriculum, and grades drive the reality of a college list. Families need to make adjustments to the college list based on this. Just like there are reach, target, and likely colleges, there are "reach students," "target students," and "likely students." I define these students as follows:

Reach students: Those who take the most challenging classes at their high school, get the strongest grades possible, and have test scores that reach the upper twenty-fifth percentile of any college, unless the student plans to apply to test-optional colleges. A reach student's college list can have reach colleges with acceptance rates of 25 percent or less, target colleges with acceptance rates between

26 and 50 percent, and likely colleges with acceptance rates of 51 percent or higher.

Target students: Those who take a mix of college prep and advanced classes (AP, IB, etc.) with grades in the A to B range, and test scores in the middle 50 percent of all their colleges. A target student should identify reach colleges with acceptance rates between 26 and 50 percent, target colleges with rates between 51 and 70 percent, and likely colleges with acceptances of 71 percent or higher.

Likely students: Those with a more standard-level curriculum, with As, Bs, and possibly some Cs (or lower) and lower test scores. Likely students should consider reach colleges as those that have acceptance rates of 51 to 70 percent; target colleges will be ones that have an acceptance rate of 70 to 80 percent; and likely colleges will have acceptance rates of 80 percent or higher.

Depending on which category the student falls into, the family must adjust the list, shifting the college categories to better match up with a student's objective criteria.

For example, if I am working with a "reach student," I provide a three-column list of reach, target, and likely schools. Take a look at a sample:

REACH COLLEGES	TARGET COLLEGES	LIKELY COLLEGES
Washington University (St. Louis)	University of Miami	Elon University
Rice University	George Washington University	Southern Methodist University
Tulane University	University of Florida	University of Pittsburgh

If the student is a "target student," then I shift the categories to the left. The original reach colleges (acceptance rates of 25 percent or less) get removed. Then the original target colleges become reach colleges, the likely colleges become targets, and I add more colleges with higher acceptance rates just to be safe for the likely college category:

REACH COLLEGES	TARGET COLLEGES	LIKELY COLLEGES
University of Miami	Elon University	James Madison University
George Washington University	Southern Methodist University	High Point University
University of Florida	University of Pittsburgh	College of Charleston

And if I am working with a "likely student," I shift things to the left even more, providing more colleges with higher acceptance rates in each category:

REACH COLLEGES	TARGET COLLEGES	LIKELY COLLEGES
Elon University	James Madison University	Barry University
Southern Methodist University	High Point University	Eckerd College
University of Pittsburgh	College of Charleston	Auburn University

As you see from every example, I have an equal number of reach, target, and likely schools. I also only have nine schools for each example. It takes a lot to narrow down a list to nine schools with an equal number in each category, but that is my goal for a final college list. Anything more can be extremely taxing on the student (and expensive). Anything less might be okay, but you just want to make sure that students can see themselves going to every college on the list no matter what category the college falls into.

THE TEN PILLARS

A sound college list can ensure that every student has plenty of acceptances and options. Just as a Soundbite is supported by nouns and verbs, the college list must have "support" as well. In putting together a starter list, balancing an intermediate list, or polishing up the final list, you need to keep the following ten pillars in mind:

1. Your Soundbite
2. Your strengths
3. Your limitations
4. Acceptance rates of each college for the most recent admissions cycle
5. Your highest SAT or ACT scores (and Subject Test scores if applicable)
6. Your curriculum from the ninth through twelfth grades
7. Your GPA and rank (if available)
8. Your top three nonnegotiables
9. Whether college visits are a priority, a possibility, or not in the cards for you
10. The pieces of the application you feel will highlight your strengths

Defining these ten pillars will keep you grounded and ensure that the colleges on your list, at whatever stage, fulfill your personal criteria while also being viable choices.

PILLAR #1: YOUR SOUNDBITE

Remember the young woman from Chapter 10 who took her advocacy skills to fight for antivaping laws in her home state? She is the same young woman who kept her Soundbite at the top of every college list she made for herself. This young woman was one of the most earnest students I have ever worked with. She took to the Soundbite concept even in the early stages.

That popular saying "Never take your eye off the prize" was her mantra. Yet I respected her so much because the "prize" was not acceptance into a certain college. The prize was living her Soundbite—she never took her eye off of her Soundbite.

The more she wrote out her Soundbite, the more it stuck. I loved her idea. It led her to a balanced list of colleges. While she had a number of highly selective colleges on the list, she had plenty of colleges that fit into the "target" and "likely" categories. We both knew that those colleges would appreciate her application. She applied to a few colleges under their Rolling Admissions programs and heard back in the fall of senior year that she was admitted to those schools.

Note, it is always a great idea to apply to a few Rolling Admissions schools very early on in senior year. It is typically easier to get admitted to a college with a Rolling Admissions program in late summer or early fall, as there is more space in the class then, rather than later in the year. Rolling Admissions colleges usually have higher acceptance rates and are oftentimes a student's "likely" choices. So if a student hears back early in the fall that they didn't get admitted to their Rolling Admissions colleges, it is usually a sign that they are overshooting and need to readjust their list to include colleges with even higher acceptance rates.

Applying to some Rolling Admissions programs gave my student peace of mind, and it can give you peace of mind too. This young woman also applied to a number of public institutions with Early Action programs as well as to a Restrictive Early Action program, Stanford University. Again, this was a really smart move. If for some reason she didn't get admitted to her "early" options, she could have adjusted her Regular Decision list to include more realistic choices before it was too late. She knew that Stanford was a reach for every student, but she had plenty of good choices on her list, so if Stanford didn't work out, she would still have viable options at the end.

Her college list and her commitment to her Soundbite worked beautifully. Stanford and plenty of other colleges admitted her. She chose Stanford in the end. But it wasn't a perfect application that led to these acceptances; it was a perfect college list based on her Soundbite that led to such extraordinary outcomes.

I saw how affirming it was for that young woman to make sure she kept her Soundbite in mind at all times—while formulating her college list through to finalizing it. Now, I encourage all of my students to do the same.

The first thing a student should do before beginning a college list is to write or type their Soundbite on their list, front and center. It is up to the student to research and ideally visit the colleges on their list to determine if each will appreciate their Soundbite. If the student is not able to do in-person visits, they can take advantage of a virtual tour and information session through the college's website or online events. The exercise at the end of this chapter will take you step-by-step through creating a college list specific to you. For the ten pillars, you must determine if each college on your starter, intermediate, and final lists matches up with your Soundbite and what is truly important to you.

PILLAR #2: YOUR STRENGTHS

Return to the Know Thyself Exercise from Chapter 5. Strengths are not just academic in nature. Some students will show particular ability or promise in an extracurricular activity or a personal skill. The more specific you can be, the better! For example, don't just say, "My strength is that I am a great writer." Instead, provide the kind of detail that allows you to be one in a million (or more).

Note that oftentimes a strength can fit under multiple categories. And in college, an extracurricular or personal strength could become an academic pursuit, and an academic strength can turn into an extracurricular or personal passion! Here are some examples:

ACADEMIC STRENGTH:

- Analytical writing or creative writing
- Lab work
- Advanced-level math
- Double-language pursuit (taking two foreign languages throughout high school)
- World geography

EXTRACURRICULAR STRENGTH:

- Music composition
- One-hundred-meter butterfly event in swimming
- In-demand tutor or babysitter
- Lighting and sound guru for all school performances
- Highest scorer on the math team

PERSONAL STRENGTH:

- Taking standardized tests
- Creating and delivering original jokes

- Trip packer extraordinaire
- Observer of people
- Grammar

I love the possibilities for all of these strengths—even the personal ones. For example, being good at telling jokes to your family and friends can turn into something much bigger—majoring in theater, participating in open-mic nights, joining an improv group, or writing an original comedic screenplay.

Or take the "observer of people" example. That was me growing up. I could watch people—yes, strangers—literally for hours whether I was at a restaurant, an airport, or even the grocery store. I was fascinated by trying to figure out each person's story. It is no surprise that I ended up becoming an admissions officer whose job it was to sift through the many stories of young people and piece together who they were. I wish I had been more self-aware as a high school and college student to recognize how much I loved figuring out people based on how they acted on their own or interacted with others. It might have saved me from going to law school!

Strengths are pliable and transferable to academic majors, extracurricular pursuits, hobbies, and ultimate careers. Be open to the possibility of taking a nontraditional strength and celebrating it in college or, ideally, sooner. For each college on your list, do your research and make sure your strengths have a home on their campus. It can be as obvious as the fact that the college has a specific academic department or extracurricular club that is in line with your strength, or it can be less obvious. In fact, just because a college doesn't have an academic major directly related to your strength or doesn't have a club on their campus just yet, that is not grounds for removing the college from the list. Colleges want what they don't have. They might value something you offer but not yet have found the right student to bring it to life! The only way to know for sure is to do research on every college on your list and find out.

PILLAR #3: YOUR LIMITATIONS

We all have them. Revisit yours from the Know Thyself Exercise. This is important because if one of your current limitations is a major component of a college's admissions process, you need to keep this in mind as you build your college list. For example, some students identify their limitation as standardized tests. Ahem, that was me in high school. However, many of these students still end up applying to colleges with exceptionally high SAT and ACT averages for the students admitted. The beautiful thing about limitations is that they don't always last forever. But, in the meantime, students should identify their limitations and make sure they are not weighed heavily in the admissions process for the colleges on their lists. Acknowledging our limitations means understanding ourselves well enough not to let those limitations get in the way of our Soundbite or goal.

PILLAR #4: ACCEPTANCE RATES

No matter what type of college list I am reviewing, I am focused on the acceptance rates. That is because these acceptance rates have less to do with the students and more to do with the competition.

A student with a 1600 SAT score, straight-A record, and tons of Advanced Placement classes is not guaranteed admission to any college these days. The most selective colleges in the country want high scores and grades, but these are simply expected of every applicant in their pools. This results in most of their decisions coming down to other parts of the application.

Students should focus on the college's acceptance rate not just before they apply but even before they visit. Most families only visit what I define as "reach" colleges. If a student does not see enough realistic "target" and "likely" colleges, their final list will tend to be dominated by reach colleges, and this can significantly reduce the number of acceptances they receive and affect the student's sense of self-worth.

Just as every college list should have a nice mix of reach, target, and likely colleges, so too should the student's visits (virtual and in person). In other words, if a student visits a reach college in a particular city or region, they should plan to visit at least one target and one likely college as well. This is absolutely necessary not only because it is important for a student to have some target and likely colleges on their list that they could see themselves attending but also because many of those target and likely colleges factor demonstrated interest into the admissions process. Doing an official campus visit is the best way to show demonstrated interest. As a result of the COVID-19 pandemic, however, virtual visits can sometimes count as demonstrated interest if the college collects students' data before they view the virtual tour or information session.

The most effective way to determine if a college is a reach, target, or likely school is to find the most recent admissions cycle's acceptance rate. I do not rely on outside sources for this. I look for data provided by the college instead of relying on a third party to supply this very important data point. The acceptance rate for the most recent class is sometimes included on the college's admissions website and is often labeled as the "Profile for the Class of [Most Recent Class]." If the college doesn't have this easily accessible, I also look at the student newspaper for an article in April or May about the college's most recent admissions cycle, but that tends to not include students admitted from the waitlist. Ultimately I often look up the number of total acceptances and divide that by the total number of applications from public data found on the college's "Common Data Set" or through the Integrated Postsecondary Education Data System.

PILLAR #5: YOUR TEST SCORES

I have been on every possible side of the admissions process. Initially, I think the best of everyone. I want to believe that everyone is telling the truth. But the one area in which AOs downplay or stretch the truth the most is test scores. They don't want to discourage students with lower scores from applying, as part of their job is to increase the number of applications each year. And most AOs also don't want to sound condescending to students with lower scores, although there are exceptions to this rule. So they often preach, "There are so many pieces to the application. Testing is not as important as most think. We focus the most attention on a student's transcript."

Sound familiar? Truth be told, this is how we were trained to speak about test scores when I was an entry-level AO. But the truth is test scores do matter, and they matter a whole lot more than AOs let on. The only way a student with lower test scores gets admitted (then and now) is if they are a "tagged" student: recruited athlete, underrepresented student, student from an underrepresented home state, or someone with connections. The regular student with lower test scores but without a "tag" will face some tough odds getting admitted to a highly selective college.

This can be a sobering exercise, but it is better to go into this process with knowledge rather than being blindsided at the end. Look at your scores and the average scores of the admitted pool of students for each college on your list. (Again, these can be found on the college's website.) This is essential in being self-aware of your current strengths and limitations.

If your highest test scores are in the top quarter or middle 50 percent of the college's average, you can include this college on the list. Scores in the bottom quarter of a college's average make this college *unlikely* unless the student's scores increase or the college has a test-optional admissions policy in which test scores are not required. Notice that I identified this college as "unlikely" for admission instead of simply a "reach" college. This is because, in this highly competitive landscape, reach colleges are only within reach if the student has the transcript and test scores to be competitive within the applicant pool.

Again, identifying which colleges are reach, target, and likely schools on your list has more to do with the college's acceptance rate. Initially, that should drive how you identify colleges first.

PILLAR #6: YOUR CURRICULUM

I often tell families that some colleges recalculate the student's unweighted GPA with just the academic core classes: English, math, history/social studies, science, and a foreign language. That makes them question if taking advanced-level classes or weighted classes at some high schools is even worth it. Is it? Absolutely.

Regardless of whether a college recalculates a GPA, the AO is trained to evaluate the rigor of the curriculum for each year of high school. In fact, when I read applications at Penn, I literally counted up the number of Advanced Placement and Honors classes for every student in every year of high school, including senior year. I then compared that to the number of Advanced Placement and Honors classes offered by the high school.

College counselors are supposed to indicate how many advanced classes are offered each year on the "school report" form they fill out. But most high schools provide a full list of these classes on what is often referred to as the "school profile," which is supposed to be updated each year to reflect the most accurate curriculum available to its students. Ask your college counselor to get a copy of your school's official profile if you cannot find it easily on your school's website. Granted, not every high school offers advanced-level classes like AP and Honors classes, and not every student is meant to take these classes. However, based on the college's acceptance rate, students can determine how their curriculum compares to what is expected from each college on their list.

For example, colleges with acceptance rates of 25 percent or less expect students to be taking the most challenging curriculum (usually in all core subjects) offered at their high school. Colleges with acceptance rates of 26 to 50 percent like to see plenty of advanced-level classes, but a student doesn't have to be taking every advanced class available. And colleges with acceptance rates over 50 percent are not as strict about the rigor of the curriculum as long as the student is meeting at least the minimum standards for admission. If the student exceeds those standards, their chances of admission increase.

PILLAR #7: YOUR GPA AND RANK

Is a student's GPA or class rank strong enough for each college? This is harder to determine. Because there are so many possible grading scales and many high schools no longer rank, colleges oftentimes don't even publish an average GPA/rank for their admitted students because they simply don't have one. However, as with the curriculum pillar, students can measure their GPA and/or rank (if available) by the following standards:

- Colleges with acceptance rates of 25 percent or less will typically admit students with recalculated GPAs (only academic core classes from ninth through eleventh grade) that end up reflecting an A or an A– average. That means that students can absolutely still get some Bs in high school, but the more they have, the tougher it will be to get admitted. If a student is aware of their class rank, being within the top 10 percent of your class is ideal—and the higher within the top 10 percent the better.

- Colleges with acceptance rates between 26 and 50 percent are looking for recalculated GPAs in the A to B range and class rank roughly in the top half of the class. Of course, a college with an acceptance rate of 27 percent is almost like a reach college, so having a rank within the top 10 percent is still ideal.

- Colleges with acceptance rates above 50 percent are more forgiving when it comes to grades. The closer their acceptance rate is to 50 percent, however, the more attention they will pay to the grades.

PILLAR #8: YOUR TOP THREE NONNEGOTIABLES (AT LEAST NOW!)

Every student goes into this college process with a few things they are looking for in a college. This is especially helpful when creating a starter list. Common nonnegotiables can be the following:

- Academic major
- Ability to play a varsity sport
- Size
- Location
- Curriculum/requirements
- Cultural opportunities
- Religious affiliation

- Type of institution (university versus liberal arts college)
- Preprofessional opportunities
- Availability of merit scholarships
- Cost
- Diversity

When identifying your top three nonnegotiables, be aware that while these factors may lead you to a conceptual match, you need to visit the campus to have a better sense of whether the college is a match in reality. I cannot tell you how many students change their minds about intended majors, location, student body size, or other popular nonnegotiables after seeing a few colleges. So, while a student should identify up to three nonnegotiables, they need to be ready when a nonnegotiable becomes negotiable. What may seem important to a student initially often changes over time, just like the Soundbite.

PILLAR #9: COLLEGE VISITS: PRIORITY, POSSIBILITY, OR NOT IN THE CARDS?

I cannot stress the importance of college visits enough. Not only do visits help determine the "match" and whether or not the student should ultimately apply, but they can mean the difference between an acceptance or a denial at some colleges. A large percentage of colleges, mostly private ones, factor "demonstrated interest" into their admissions process. This means that they evaluate how interested a student is in them when determining the admissions decision. There are a number of ways to show a college demonstrated interest. The most powerful way is to do an official college visit through the admissions office (in person if possible or virtually at the very least).

If you want to figure out if a college uses demonstrated interest in the admissions process, look at the college's most recent Common Data Set, which is typically published by the school's institutional research department. Under First-Year/Freshman Admissions, a chart allows a college to check off what it factors into the admissions process. If "level of applicant's interest" is "considered" at a minimum, a student should try to prioritize a college visit unless there are financial limitations for that student.

There are other, more personally driven reasons why students should visit the colleges on their list. Most selective colleges will require specific essays to apply. These essays, commonly called supplemental essays as they often appear on a college's supplement to the Common Application or Co-alition Application, can be straightforward and require the student to answer why they are applying to that specific college. Other essay prompts can be subtler: "Talk about a time, in or outside the classroom, when you worked with others and what you learned from the experience." No matter what, understanding the values and educational philosophy of each college on your list is absolutely necessary to being able to write these extra essays. Students can pick up on what a college values from the website, but nothing is as helpful in writing these essays as visiting.

When I worked in the Penn Admissions Office, I could tell just by reading the supplemental essay if the student had visited the campus or not. We didn't track visitors. It didn't matter. Students who had visited could evoke feelings and impressions of Penn in their essay, while students who hadn't visited often relied on common buzzwords and themes found on the university's website.

If college visits are not in the cards or you are not able to visit all of the schools on your list before applying, you may want to consider including more colleges that don't factor in demonstrated interest. And you might want to avoid colleges that don't have extra, supplemental essays too. But if you have the time and resources to visit colleges, do it! Visiting colleges is the only way to know if you should even apply, let alone enroll there.

Starting early can be helpful. If you want to visit all of the colleges before you apply, starting visits sooner rather than later can help. Families of younger students can visit schools whenever they are ready—that can be as early as ninth or tenth grade. Any long weekend can turn into a mini college tour. And if you are like me, every place we visit as a family, I take my kids to visit at least one college. I want them to see and dream of the possibilities in front of them.

PILLAR #10: THE PIECES OF THE APPLICATION YOU FEEL HIGHLIGHT YOUR STRENGTHS

I often share that I went into college counseling because I had very little formal help when I was going through the admissions process. Luckily, I had my very invested father by my side. We learned together. But one of the most important things he did was point me in the direction of smaller colleges. Not only could I be a big fish in a small pond in that type of environment, but almost every small liberal arts college offers (still to this day!) on-campus evaluative interviews. The interview was a place for me to shine. It was a hint at what I would major in (communication) and what I would do for a living (public speaking).

It is a reminder to seek out colleges that will value you and what you can bring to their campuses and communities. If you are an exceptional writer, you should be considering colleges that require additional essays and possibly even encourage writing portfolios. Applying to colleges without a required essay might make your life easier, but it flies in the face of who you are. Below are a few examples of strengths that can correspond with certain aspects of a college application:

STRENGTH	APPLICATION COMPONENT
Writing	Main essay, supplemental essays, and potential writing portfolio
Interpersonal skills (good in an interview setting!)	On-campus evaluative interviews by an admissions staff member (as opposed to an alumni interview, which factors in very little); optional or required video submissions
Relationships with teachers	One or two required recommendation letters from academic teachers
Strong test taker	SAT/ACT scores
Strong transcript	Test-optional policy
Athletics	Recruitment for varsity sports

The whole idea of Soundbite is to home in on something that truly sets you apart. The more specific you can get with your Soundbite, the more you stand out. But remember that not everyone or every college will appreciate your Soundbite. Being self-aware allows you to control your college list, which leads to your dictating whether you get admitted or not. Without self-awareness, the student's process moves out of their control and gives all of the power to the colleges. Don't let that happen. Self-awareness will help you create the most sound college list, and it will guide you through every chapter of your life.

COLLEGE LIST EXERCISE

Step 1: Identify what type of student you are and circle it.

Reach student

This is a student who is getting mostly As or A–'s in the most challenging curriculum (in all five core subjects) offered at the high school and has test scores, if available, in the top twenty-fifth percentile at most colleges (ACT: 34–36; SAT: 1520–1600).

Target student

This is a student who takes some but not all advanced-level classes, gets As and Bs, and has test scores in the middle 50 percent of all their colleges.

Likely student

This is a student with a more standard-level curriculum, with As, Bs, and possibly some Cs (or lower) and lower test scores.

Step 2: Identify your pillars. Fill in your responses in the right-hand column.

PILLAR	ANSWER
Your Soundbite:	
Your strengths:	
Your limitations:	

PILLAR	ANSWER
Acceptance rates for each college category based on your being a reach, target, or likely student: (Example for a reach student: Reach: 25 percent or less Target: 26–50 percent Likely: 51 percent or higher)	
Highest SAT or ACT score:	
Type of curriculum you take: (Most challenging, very challenging, or standard college prep)	
Your GPA and rank (if available):	
Top three nonnegotiables:	
College visits: (Priority, possibility, or "not in the cards" for most of your colleges)	
The pieces of the application you feel highlight your strengths:	

Step 3: Create a starter list of colleges. First put your Soundbite at the top of your list!

This is ideal for a ninth and tenth grader or for an eleventh or twelfth grader who is just getting started. Always make sure to have just as many target and likely colleges as you have reach colleges.

List your Soundbite here:

_____

_____

_____

_____

REACH COLLEGES	TARGET COLLEGES	LIKELY COLLEGES

Step 4: Does every college on your starter list meet your pillars? Remove any that do not.

_____

_____

_____

_____

Step 5: Build your intermediate college list after doing further research and visiting more colleges. Put your Soundbite at the top of your list! Note that the intermediate list is often longer than the starter list.

List your Soundbite here:

_____

_____

_____

_____

REACH COLLEGES	TARGET COLLEGES	LIKELY COLLEGES

Step 6: Does each college on your intermediate list fulfill your pillars? Remove any that do not.

_____

_____

_____

_____

Step 7: The ideal final college list includes between nine and twelve colleges for most students. Make sure not to forget to put your Soundbite at the top of your list!

List your Soundbite here:

_____

_____

_____

_____

REACH COLLEGES	TARGET COLLEGES	LIKELY COLLEGES

Step 8: Does each college on the final list meet your pillars? Remove any that do not.

_____

_____

_____

_____

Step 9: Do you have at least one Rolling Admissions and an Early Action (and possibly an Early Decision) option on your list? If not, add or replace colleges to create as many early acceptances as possible.

_____

_____

_____

CHAPTER 12

The Homegrown Idea

I admit to being a part of the "sign-my-kid-up" parenting generation. Swim lessons, tennis clinics, homework helpers, and, for some families, camps. You name it, we've either participated in one of these options as a student or paid for them as a parent. Some of these experiences are worth their weight in gold as they teach young people valuable life skills, like learning how to swim or how to study for tests. Others end up being an indulgence, sometimes even an unnecessary one. Either way, it is fairly painless, cost aside. Sign up, pay the fee, and the child will get a structured experience that can deliver improved skills or measurable outcomes at the very least, as long as the student is committed to it.

But along the way, parents and children alike have become reliant on these structured, sometimes manufactured experiences. When it comes to high school, the sign-me-up mentality explodes with hundreds of clubs, teams, and organizations students can audition for, try out for, or simply just join.

Interested in community service? Join your school's Key Club or a similarly focused service-oriented club.

Want to play ultimate Frisbee? Become a member of the school's club ultimate Frisbee team.

Want to develop your science interest? Sign up for the science club or possibly even get a job working at a laboratory at a local university.

These are all well within a student's grasp. Parents applaud the opportunity as a chance to show colleges how interested and invested their child is in a particular field. Students see it as a chance to get hands-on experience in a field or extracurricular activity that they might pursue in college. The logic makes sense. There is usually zero (or very little) cost involved, and it provides varying levels of evidence of a student's intentions and plans for the future.

Yet, as the college admissions process became more competitive over the last several decades, parents wanted their child to go one step further in order to stand out. Doing "sign-me-up" clubs, joining school sports' teams, or working a traditional summer job just didn't feel like enough. Parents were willing to shell out significant money and travel miles for their child to experience something more, during both the school year and the summer break. Club sports teams grew exponentially, attracting athletes from tristate areas to practice and compete on a higher level. And colleges saw a similar opportunity to maximize the "sign-my-kid-up" generation. Parents were willing to pay for almost anything. With pressure to increase revenue, especially during the summer months, when room and board fees come to a halt or significantly slow down, colleges have turned their campuses into playgrounds for high school students.

Johns Hopkins University *pioneered* this field when it founded the Center for Talented Youth (CTY) in 1979. CTY was the first to offer academic summer programs to middle and high school kids at college campuses around the country. It was a win-win-*win* situation for all involved. CTY charged hundreds of dollars (now thousands) for students to spend part of their summer with them; the colleges got a sizable check for allowing CTY to use their dorms and facilities; and the students believed that they got an edge in the admissions process.

Now, over forty years later, most colleges, especially the more selective ones, offer multiple summer programs geared toward high school students. Students can take mock "college" classes, live in the dorms, and experience a taste of what it is like to attend that particular college, or college in general. Tens of thousands of students participate in these programs every summer. They range in cost from several hundreds of dollars for a short program at a local college to upward of $13,000 to spend the summer at Harvard University. And for-profit travel and excursion organizations have also jumped on the bandwagon, offering teen trips domestically and overseas, costing thousands of dollars. All of these programs boast that these experiences can enhance a student's chances of admission. But in fact, any program that costs money, regardless of how selective it is, can hurt a student's chances—even, in some cases, at the college hosting the summer program. What often gets overlooked is the fact that the college's admissions office has no involvement or investment in the program and, in fact, may often veer as far away from it as possible.

Because these programs suggest privilege—both in terms of the student's knowledge of them and ability to pay for them—admissions officers are trained to view them with a critical eye. When I was a newly minted AO, I was instructed to be on the lookout for these programs on a student's application. Attending a pay-to-play program—or, more aptly, reporting it on the application—is risky if you are considering highly selective colleges. And the same goes for the student who writes about one of these pay-to-play programs in an essay. Just don't do it.

There are exceptions to this rule, which I will review later in this chapter. However, it is essential not to rely solely on sign-me-up clubs, and it is plain risky to associate pay-to-play programs with acceptances to highly selective colleges. Almost any student can be a member of a club or take part in one of these programs, and this makes the experience more common. The bolder and much more challenging move is to do something no one else is doing. That is where the homegrown idea begins.

At the root of the homegrown idea is a student's Soundbite and their own ingenuity. For example, they might be interested in an area that is academic in nature or an extracurricular pursuit (or both), and they have the creativity, courage, and discipline to go out on a limb and build something from the ground up. The most obvious example of this is when a student creates a new club at their high school, starts their own business, or launches a nonprofit organization. There are hoops to jump through; vision is needed and sacrifice involved. Being a founder of a new endeavor is impressive. But being a *pioneer* is something even more extraordinary.

The difference between a founder and a pioneer is subtle at first. A student who hears about a club at a neighboring high school and brings that same club to their high school is a founder. What makes her a pioneer is if she creates a club that has never been created by anyone and brings it to her community, grows it, and has a national voice on the subject matter. A founder creates opportunity for herself and those immediately around her. A pioneer makes an impact on the greater world.

The same approach can be applied to a student founding his own business or nonprofit organization. Twenty years ago, it was unusual for a high school student to do this. Today, it is not as unusual. That said, this student is a founder, and quite accomplished at that. But if he wants to be a pioneer, his concept and impact must be novel in some way and should change the way something is done or yield uncommon results. The biggest challenge for this student is accomplishing these feats in a short amount of time. Any founder will tell you that it typically takes years to see measurable results. I can personally attest to this myself.

That is why the sooner a student has the courage to do something that no one else is doing, the more time she has to develop her homegrown idea, grow it, and see uncommon results. I wish I'd had the courage to create a homegrown idea as a high school student. I just followed the crowd. I joined the tennis team because that's what my dad told me I should do; I tried out for the musical, not because I could sing but because my friends were doing it; and I passively joined other clubs as a member. I was the most uninspired member of the Spanish Club, National Honor Society, and Model Congress. It was not until my freshman year of college that I started recognizing that playing tennis made me miserable and that while I couldn't sing, I had this surprising love for speaking in front of large groups—the larger, the better. When I took a pivot away from tennis (yes, that's my lingo instead of using the word "quit"), I had time to practice my public speaking as a tour guide for the college's admissions office to quench my growing obsession with the college admissions process. So there was no homegrown idea just yet, and geez, do I regret not starting sooner.

This chapter is a lesson in self-awareness, confidence, and timing. Back in high school, I did not think I had the pioneer gene. But, in fact, we all have it. The gene is part of our DNA. We just have to be open to uncovering it and diving headfirst into something foreign to our normal tendencies of blending in. Standing out is everything.

Here are a few examples of homegrown ideas. These were real ideas I gave to students I worked with. They chose not to pursue them for a variety of reasons—sometimes because it was too much work in their eyes and oftentimes because of a lack of interest or motivation. There's a reason for the sign-me-up approach: it is a whole lot easier to join something already in place than to create something from nothing. The rewards of the latter are far greater, though. I have listed the homegrown idea, the potential Soundbite if the student had chosen to pursue it, and the real Soundbite that resulted from the student choosing the more expected path:

STUDENT #1: THE FILMMAKER

Homegrown idea: Create your own film, on your own with every free moment you have starting right now (eleventh grade!).

> Student's Potential Soundbite: For the past year, I wrote, directed, starred in, and edited my own film, which taught me more about filmmaking—the struggles and triumphs—than anything else because it was up to me to make my vision a reality.

Actual idea: Attended a one-week pay-to-play film program right before senior year where a film was made for the final project with four other members of the group.

> Student's Soundbite: I didn't get to write the screenplay or to direct or edit it, but I had a role in the film that we created at a pay-to-play program.

STUDENT #2: THE PREMED STUDENT WHO LOVES GERMAN

Homegrown idea: Study the great German scientists and their original papers in German to uncover insights into scientific discovery, the German language, and how their approach influenced modern science.

> Student's Potential Soundbite: I study the German language and the early German scientists, ultimately translating Albert Einstein's "Annus Mirabilis" papers from German to English to understand science through his mind.

Actual idea: This student attended the pay-to-play National Youth Leadership Forum on Medicine with thousands of other students across the country just like him.

> Student's Soundbite: I want to study science and go to med school, so I attended a program called the National Youth Leadership Forum on Medicine with thousands of other students just like me.

STUDENT #3: THE NYC WRITER WHO LOVES SEEING PLAYS ON BROADWAY

Homegrown idea: Create a blog for students who don't live close to NYC or have the resources to see plays in order to make Broadway truly accessible to all.

> Student's Potential Soundbite: I know how lucky I am to live in NYC and see Broadway shows, and I want to bring this magic to my peers through a weekly blog that expands Broadway supporters and audiences one kid at a time.

Actual idea: Chose to attend the New York Times Summer Academy for four weeks in the summer (cost: $11,650) instead of sharing his passion through his own homegrown idea.

> Student's Soundbite: I attended the prestigious New York Times Summer Academy, and even though it was a really expensive program, it was sponsored by the *New York Times*—impressive, right?

Wrong. As impressive as the National Youth Leadership Forum on Medicine and the New York Times Summer Academy sound to families, these are traditional pay-to-play programs. There might be financial aid available, but the truth is that students can create a much more self-driven project on their own if they pursue a homegrown idea. It is always more impressive to create rather than to buy a premade kit ready to go for as many students who want to pay for it.

While some students have no interest in pursuing the homegrown idea, there are plenty of students who do:

- The student who had an interest in fashion and started his own styling business when friends and family members started asking him for fashion advice. (University of Southern California)
- The engineering applicant who lived in the mountains and created a "Snow Day Predictor" for her small town. (Stevens Institute of Technology)
- The photographer who took pictures of individuals often overlooked by society and spent the last two years of high school taking and editing a series of photographs of the homeless, laborers, and mothers, which culminated in a stand-alone exhibit at her high school during her senior year. (University of Michigan)
- The oldest of seven children, the last three of whom were adopted and addicted to opium at birth, who conducted statistical and sociological research on birth mothers and opium addiction. (Dartmouth College)
- The creator, blogger, and YouTube star behind a series that helps American teenagers understand math. (Massachusetts Institute of Technology)
- The spearfisher who risked her life in the choppy seas of the Pacific to address food insecurities for the elderly on her island. (High school student)
- The student who created a nonprofit organization dedicated to offering dance classes, dance shoes, and dance clothing to children unable to dance due to cost or a lack of access. (University of Notre Dame)

The homegrown idea need not be as far-reaching as one might think. Sometimes the homegrown idea never makes it out of the student's community; yet the potential is there for greater impact after the college admissions process, if not before. Once a student realizes the power of his own idea, he understands that it can be replicated or developed further. Just as the Soundbite concept evolves and changes over time, so too does a student's interests. But with a proven track record of creating one homegrown idea, a student knows he can do it again.

The beauty of the homegrown idea is twofold. First, because no one else is doing it or, in some cases, has ever done it, the student does not have to live up to someone else's achievements. Whatever they accomplish is determined by them. As much as it is great to reach the pinnacle of an industry (like a writer getting a book published), the success of a homegrown idea is measured in the hours, weeks, and years of building it, which matter more than an end goal. The little successes along the way become part of the student's story and add up to an inspiring Soundbite that moves others.

The other wondrous piece of the homegrown idea is that if you are the pioneer and the only one to start it, there is no competition—no peers to beat out or rise above. It's not like trying to become the starting quarterback of your high school football team and having to outperform five other players for the same position or having to run for a school club office in order to gain that one big leadership title that admissions officers weigh more than others. When you are the pioneer, you inspire others to join you, which makes the potential for a positive contribution even greater.

The alternative to the homegrown idea is to outperform everyone else around you in a specialty, sport, art, or other pursuit. You know those individuals. They exist, but their achievements are uncommon and elusive for most. Like the student who wins the national science fair, the student who goes to the Olympics and gets recruited to play that sport in college, or the national Future Business Leaders of America winner. These students are doing activities that show up in almost every high school or community. But they are so extraordinarily talented in a particular area that their achievement overshadows everyone else doing that same activity. You can try to compete with them and beat them at their own game, but that's hard to do. They are successful in the college admissions world because they are viewed as the absolute best (not one of the best) in the more traditional pursuits. So students have a choice: try to compete with the best in the more traditional activities or create their own homegrown idea that allows them to be the best at something just as extraordinary yet nontraditional. Either option becomes the foundation of a truly distinctive, powerful, and inspiring Soundbite. Which path will you choose?

Finally, I mentioned earlier in this chapter that there are exceptions to the rule for pay-to-play programs. Faculty members at colleges usually have very little or no involvement with these summer programs and the freshman admissions selection process. However, performing arts and fine arts faculty often have a larger role in the summer program and the selection of freshmen. Students who are interested in conservatory performing arts or the fine arts may find value in these programs.

And it is important to mention that some fully funded summer programs are highly respected by admissions officers. Hopefully a student does one of these programs because it supports their Soundbite. But they are absolutely not necessary.

Students don't have to wait until the summertime or count on a structured program to make an impact. In fact, those students who start pursuing a homegrown idea earlier in high school have the time to develop it and see it come to life. That is when the time invested and the small and large achievements of the homegrown idea transcend the typical application and exemplify what it means to be a pioneer.

One last note about homegrown projects concerns the proliferation of college consultants with little or no formal college admissions experience working with high school students. I have heard way too many college consultants marketing their services to help students develop a "passion project." This may sound similar to my "homegrown project" terminology. The difference comes down to authenticity. When the idea or project is born from a natural curiosity and pursuit of knowledge or impact, it feels organic, homegrown, and innate to the student. When it is orchestrated by someone who has never read applications as a full-time admissions officer or made final decisions on applications as a senior leader of an admissions team, it rarely rings true. Ultimately, the best ideas come from the student. The best ideas are driven by the student. The best ideas have the most potential to contribute not just to a college application but to the world around us.

CHAPTER 13

The Special-Special

I call Philadelphia my hometown. I was born there. I lived there during my twenties. And I still return as often as I can. It is a place of extraordinary contrast. Historic and cutting-edge. Refinement mixed with rabid fans. Beauty and grit. In my first admissions job at the University of Pennsylvania, I learned to appreciate contrast on a deep and intellectual level. One of Penn's pillars always struck me as "so Philadelphia." The undergraduate focus has been, and always will be, interdisciplinary in nature, meaning that the curriculum is meant to encourage students to explore connections between multiple academic disciplines. Penn is not alone. Many colleges have adopted this interdisciplinary mantra as well.

And even admissions officers who themselves received a very narrow undergraduate education, focused on just one academic discipline with few classes outside that field, quickly appreciate that the students who make connections across disciplines are ready to jump into that interdisciplinary environment they are trying to promote.

On an undergraduate level, this generates the student who might want to double major. But it's more than that. It's the student who creates their own individualized major. It's the student who does cutting-edge research in their unusual intersecting area of disciplines. It's the student who takes their idea and launches it to market. It's the student who becomes the next great filmmaker, entrepreneur, social activist, scientific researcher . . .

Interdisciplinary in the context of education allows a student to see connections between two academic fields. These fields can be related, like neuroscience and psychology, dance and theater, math and statistics. But they can also be seemingly unrelated: physics and dance, history and medicine, sociology and business. It was inspiring to see these combinations come to life in students' applications to Penn. This made me want to explore my own combination several years later with my experience in college admissions and my love for communication.

I call these combinations the "special-special." It reminds me a little of the "Philly Special," the play that won the Super Bowl for the Philadelphia Eagles in 2018. Truth be told, every time I say "special-special," I think about the culinary combination Philadelphia is known for, the cheesesteak "with Whiz," of course. That's Cheez Whiz, if you are wondering. If you have ever had a Philadelphia cheesesteak "with Whiz," you know the power of a "special-special." The combination of thinly sliced beef and perfectly melted Cheez Whiz makes the Philadelphia cheesesteak so special-special, in my humble opinion. It sounds silly to refer to cheesesteaks made with Cheez Whiz as an illustration, but one can find inspiration almost anywhere. A special-special doesn't have to combine two formal academic disciplines. Hobbies, activities, and talents are all up for grabs.

Let's consider my own special-special. I love, love, love to speak publicly. Give me an audience, and I get a natural high from giving a speech. I also love, love, love the college admissions process. I have devoted my entire adult life to the process (except for that one year of law school!). As an admissions officer and dean, I was able to combine these two passions together on a daily basis. I gave a speech of some sort almost every day, be it leading an information session for visiting families, speaking at convocation at the beginning of the school year, or making a presentation to the Board of Trustees.

It wasn't until I was home for a few years with three kids under the age of seven that I started making short informational videos about getting into college from my parked car in the driveway. And now, I have a bigger audience with my Facebook Live sessions, Instagram Lives, and Application Nation video calls. At the heart of my special-special are the two things I am most passionate about, and when combined, they become my biggest strength.

And, not surprisingly, my special-special is at the root of my Soundbite: I am America's College Counselor. My special-special gives me the platform to live my Soundbite every single day.

But why wait until you get to college or even later to create your own special-special? Start now and you won't regret it. You don't need money. You just need motivation and ingenuity to create a special-special.

One of my students reminded me of the power of a special-special. This young woman has an uncanny ability to break down very complex ideas and theories for anyone. She explained to me how she researched and helped to implement a new computer application for a county office where she lives. She did this as a summer job, no less. I thought to myself, this young woman can do anything, and she can explain anything. If I can understand this and I am one of the least tech-savvy individuals on earth, she can explain anything to anyone.

Days after meeting her for the first time, she told me that she had taken her local tutoring service to the next level during the COVID-19 pandemic.

Instead of just students from her community benefiting from her academic skills, any child across the country could get free online tutoring from her or one of her colleagues amid the backdrop of school closures and the challenges of virtual learning.

When my daughter was struggling to teach herself algebra, I reached out to my student. She was happy to help. It took my daughter several days to agree to work with a tutor she didn't know, but it only took one thirty-five-minute session for her to have an entirely new perspective on a unit she was being tested on in a matter of days.

My student didn't give my daughter the answers on the study guide she was supposed to complete before her test. She just explained the concepts in a way that my daughter understood. Thirty-five minutes with a seventeen-year-old high school junior did wonders for my daughter's confidence and knowledge. She emerged from that session with confidence to fill out the study guide on her own, and a few days later got a ninety-nine on her math test.

This student is light-years ahead of her peers in terms of communication skills—that's one special thing about her. I have never interacted with anyone, let alone a high school student, who was so clear in explaining complicated ideas. It is like she can illuminate knowledge within us that we didn't even know we had.

The other special thing about this young woman is that she is especially skilled at math. As a high school student, she competed on the state level in math competitions. But it was her extraordinary communication skills, combined with a high-level math ability, that ultimately translated into a highly successful online tutoring service during a moment in our history when students needed it most.

The impact of a special-special is that the student doesn't necessarily have to be the best in the world at each of its components. It is the combination of the two things that becomes exponentially more powerful. This allows the student to do something more extraordinary than simply just pursuing each special pursuit independently. When the two are combined, the impact is far greater than the student ever dreamed.

As impressive as this student is in the aforementiond example, she was not winning national math competitions. She didn't need to. She is self-aware and realized that combining her math skills with her communication skills to form the online tutoring site/service during a critical moment created a reach far greater than just an individual achievement. That is the power of a special-special.

Here are some more examples of special-specials:

- The student who wants to major in nursing and public health and also writes for his school newspaper. Two interests: one is academic in nature (nursing), while the other is an extracurricular activity (journalism). His special-special brings these two interests together when he writes about health issues, such as mental health in teenagers. After writing for his school newspaper, he got a monthly column in his local paper. His reach expanded from his high school to his greater community. The special-special is all about expanding your reach. (Georgetown University)

- The student who speaks Arabic as a first-generation Egyptian-Turkish American. He ultimately wants to become a physician who works in war-torn regions of the world, specifically the Middle East. He plans to major in Middle Eastern studies in college in order to understand the history, culture, and people of this region. He took his bilingual skills and put them to use by volunteering with Syrian refugees in his community. His ability to speak Arabic wasn't something he deliberately set out to do; it was part of his upbringing. Yet he took this skill and applied it to the service work that he did as an extracurricular activity helping refugees navigate the medical, legal, and educational systems in their adopted home of America. Natural skill combined with volunteer work translated into a special-special with impact felt far beyond himself. (Columbia University)

- The student who dives into the complex historical relationship between Mexico and the United States and studies how this impacts the political landscape on a national level—hoping to be the first Mexican American president someday. (High school student)
- The student and pilot who takes her love for the German language and the engineering of German aircraft and serves as a docent and expert at her local aviation museum. (High school student)
- The young scientist who studies biology and fertility treatments and how she can help the LGBTQ+ community in the future. (High school student)
- The runner who uses the sport as a form of communication in teaching young girls about the power of education. (Northwestern University)

Here are some rules to live by when it comes to the special-special:

1. You don't have to be the best at something. All you need to do is see the potential in combining two things into a special-special that will allow you to make a unique impact.
2. Start small. Start from home. Start local. The power of the special-special is that if no one else has identified the combination, your idea will grow.
3. Just like the homegrown idea, the special-special is a natural way to live your Soundbite.

4. The two skills, passions, or interests can relate to each other or be absolutely, diametrically different. It's the intersection of the two components that becomes so special-special.

5. The special-special can turn into a business, a double major, an individualized major, a research focus, a social media movement, or anything else you want to pursue as an educational focus in college, as a career, or simply as a hobby.

Ultimately, the special-special goes beyond yourself. It encourages self-awareness and generosity to all who are watching. It translates into something far greater than individual achievement, college acceptance, or personal success. The special-special has the power and potential to enrich communities, solve societal problems, and help you and others grow. You can be a member or a founder. But being a pioneer takes your ideas to the next level.

CHAPTER 14

The Pivot

I spent years of my life feeling bad about quitting certain activities, leaving jobs I was miserable doing, and dropping classes that I was no longer enjoying. The list was long. Like when I no longer wanted to take ballet at eight years old or piano lessons at ten years old. Or when I quit the tennis team or decided to discontinue taking Spanish in college because another semester of grammar would make my head explode. But the biggest disappointment I brought to many was dropping out of law school—or *quitting* law school, as some would say.

Like most, I was just trying to test things out. I wanted to figure out not only what I was best at but what I enjoyed. Yet my parents were baby boomers. Stability, security, and structure were valued.

Looking back on it, my elementary, middle, and high school journey was very prescribed. Society expected me to do the activities of my gender, socioeconomic background, and religion. And since science wasn't my strength and I wouldn't be going to medical school, law school was the next best thing.

No one who knew me would say I was a rebel growing up. Rather, I was a rule follower. I tried to do what my parents wanted me to do. I didn't party. I didn't do anything that would risk my safety. I associated rebels with rule breaking rather than just living life the way one wanted. But college gave me some gumption I didn't know I had.

The first week of college, I quit the tennis team. I wanted to audition for a play. I thought I had a shot of getting a speaking role. I had been so frustrated in high school because the only performances my school did were musicals, and my singing voice was a far cry from my speaking voice. I was determined to do something I wanted to do.

And I took that word "quit" and replaced it with the word "pivot" the moment I got my first role in college—which was the only role in the play. It was just me on stage, performing my heart out in a one-woman show. I no longer wanted to be defined as the tennis player; I wanted to be the actress. *Pivot*.

My second semester of my freshman year, I applied to become a tour guide in the admissions office. I gave every tour they asked me to give in the snow, sleet, and rain. I even stayed on campus to give tours that first summer because I couldn't pry myself away from the office. I felt like I was in my element, talking to prospective families and showing them around a college that had opened up so many doors for me. I still did a play every semester, but my Soundbite was shifting. Actress, to tour guide, to admissions intern by senior year. *Pivot*.

When I told my parents I wanted to become an admissions officer, they asked, "What about law school?" *Pivot*.

So I went to law school and hated it. It was the first time in my life that I didn't enjoy school. All I could think about was becoming an admissions officer. But I didn't think I had the courage to leave. The sad part was that I was going into debt to attend law school. I had to take out loans to attend a program I had no interest in. The final straw came during the beginning of my second year of law school. I knew that I had until two weeks into the first semester before I had to take out another loan to pay for the rest of the school year. On the fourteenth day, I walked into the dean's office, formally submitted my withdrawal, and never returned. *Pivot*.

For the next twenty plus years, I embraced the pivot in large and small ways. My Soundbite changed with every pivot I was forced or chose to make. From admissions officer, to dean of admissions, to stay-at-home mom, to director of college counseling at a high school, to business owner, to America's College Counselor. That five-letter word, "pivot," has gotten me through some dark times in my life and allowed me to see myself in a positive light even when others didn't see my potential.

I am not a psychologist. I am not a spiritual leader. I am a regular girl from New Jersey who has learned to pivot at times when it would have been easy to give up. We need to change the dialogue in our homes, in our schools, and in the greater world for the younger generation. Our youth must see opportunity when they want or need to do something differently.

Pivot is a powerful tool in life. For the events that we anticipate and the many more that come as a surprise, our kids need to know how to recognize when a pivot is not only helpful but absolutely necessary for their success, well-being, and fulfillment.

The key move in the pivot has to do with substituting one thing with another. In other words, the power of the pivot is lost if we do not take the necessary steps to fill that void we are leaving behind with something more meaningful. It is not a pivot unless you fill your time, every last waking moment you can, to live your new Soundbite.

Here are some inspiring pivots of students I know:

- The young man who saw himself as a math student until he got to a huge STEM-focused magnet high school. He saw an opening with Greek as one of the only students at his high school to take the ancient language. Over the course of his four years of high school, he competed in classical-language competitions and ended up writing a story in Greek on his own. *Pivot.* (Harvard University)
- The former student athlete who took his love of football and statistics and became his school's state-winning football team's head statistician. *Pivot.* (UCLA)
- The student who was all set to intern for a physical therapist (PT) in his hometown in the summer of 2020 to complete his final set of training hours for his high school's specialty program before COVID-19 canceled everything. He was able to adapt the internship and earn his hours that summer as his grandfather's "virtual hands" in his remote PT sessions for his neurological therapy for Alzheimer's. *Pivot.* (High school student)
- The student who took the SAT over and over again without seeing the results she was hoping for. Instead of wasting more time on another test, she decided to apply to some test-optional colleges that did not require standardized tests for admission. Her powerful transcript, recommendation letters, activities list, and essay became the focal point of her application instead of scores that she felt didn't represent her fully. The test-optional colleges responded with more offers than she imagined. *Pivot.* (That's me and millions of others who didn't let test scores define them!)

The pivot can be applied to a new activity, new list of colleges, new college choice, new job, new major, new business idea, new venture, new you.

The pivot helps us evolve as individuals. The pivot helps our Soundbites evolve too. We will all face adversity, hiccups, failure, and disappointment in our lives. Handling these moments is one step. But being able to pivot is the ultimate expression of living. Living to survive. Living to thrive. Living your Soundbite.

CHAPTER 15

Decisions

Living by your Soundbite takes commitment. It is so easy to be distracted by what everyone else is doing or what everyone else wants you to do. Those who embrace their Soundbite and let it guide them every day don't fall victim to peer pressure, unreasonable parental pressure, or societal pressure.

Soundbite isn't just about getting into college. Soundbite is a lifelong mantra. It helps us make the most important decisions of our lives, and where to go to college is just one of those decisions.

The three traits to the Soundbite approach from Part 1 of this book are just as relevant in deciding where to go to college. Self-awareness, intentionality, and storytelling become guideposts for students to ensure they make the right decision for themselves.

I grew up during the popularity of the *US News & World Report's Best Colleges* series. The rankings loomed over my tiny world like a storm cloud that followed me around during my senior year of high school. I already felt like I was doomed. I was interested in small liberal arts colleges that no one from my town had ever heard of. My guidance counselor (we didn't have college counselors back then at my high school) didn't even know the schools on my list. Students who went to college from my high school attended one of the local universities.

But I forged on, applied to these seemingly no-name colleges, and ended up enrolling at one of them. Some people have heard about Hamilton College, my alma mater. Most people don't know it, though. It wasn't as highly ranked as it is now; it wasn't well known in 1993. But it was the right place for me. I knew it was because it gave me an environment that encouraged growth—intellectual, social, and personal.

I didn't have a Soundbite when I was a senior in high school. But I had enough sense about myself to know that I couldn't follow my classmates to a large state university. I'd get swallowed up. I needed a smaller, more sheltered environment, at least as an eighteen-year-old. I was not going to end up at an Ivy League university either. I didn't have the test scores to get admitted. And when a highly ranked all-women's college waitlisted me, I didn't even flinch. I refused to stay on the waitlist. I wasn't ready for the academic environment there, and in the end I wanted a traditional co-ed college experience. Knowing what you want and what you don't want is empowering, even if the decision-making process is scary.

Knowing your strengths and your own limitations (Chapter 5) is one of the first steps of the Soundbite Exercise. Once your Soundbite is in place, the self-awareness trait is activated (if it wasn't already), and it needs to stay active throughout life. Reminding ourselves about our strengths and limitations and where these thrive or fester is an important exercise as a student stares down their college acceptances.

Strengths and limitations in this final step of the college process first have to do with your own, not those of the colleges. If the strengths and limitations you identified in Chapter 5 are still accurate, they should be considered. But new strengths and limitations should also be identified. Things can change about ourselves and the world around us, and we must always be willing to adapt and evolve.

During the spring of 2020, when COVID-19 hit, high school seniors around the country were faced with making final decisions without having visited all of their choices. Additionally, many families became increasingly concerned about a number of factors. Even if cost was not a limitation when students began the college admissions process, it quickly became a limitation for many.

The pandemic reminded me that openness to the pivot is one of the best qualities to carry with you, no matter what stage of life you are in. Being in the moment of great challenge, change, and adversity is the biggest test of all. My students have taught me that we are not defined by these moments. We define ourselves by how we respond, adapt, and pivot when everything around us seems uncertain.

For the student whose financial status has changed after being admitted, reach out to your admissions officer for guidance on what to do. If the financial aid office is separate from the admissions office (and it often is), your AO will encourage you to reach out to a financial aid officer who can share what steps to take to receive more financial aid. Your AO is usually the first point of contact if you are looking for more merit aid as well.

While colleges do not like to admit this, they are being forced by the economy and determined families to make adjustments to need-based financial aid offers and merit scholarships too. You just have to ask to get the ball rolling. And if the admissions officer or financial aid officer doesn't get back to you or gets back to you with nothing better to offer, it usually is a sign to seek out other opportunities. Just as much as a student needs to show love to a college during the admissions process, the college needs to show the student just as much love after admitting them. The love needs to be mutual. If it isn't, that college doesn't deserve you.

If the student needs or wants to take time off after graduating from high school before starting college, they can request a gap year at the college where they have paid a deposit. There were more gap year requests submitted and approved after the pandemic, but it still is not as common as one might think. However, most colleges are very open to a student's request as long as they have a realistic and productive plan in place for the gap year and submit their proposal on time for approval (which is usually sometime in late spring or early summer).

And if the student decides they made a wrong decision about their undergraduate program or even their college choice, nothing is ever set in stone. While some colleges have strict rules when it comes to internal transfers from one undergraduate program to another (like going from an arts and sciences program to the business program at the same university), many are surprisingly flexible. And transferring from one institution to another is not the end of the world. My brother did it. My most trusted colleague did it. And millions of other students have done it. When your Soundbite evolves, transferring to a different program or a different college is sometimes the best pivot you can make. But one must be self-aware to recognize this.

The miraculous thing about strengths and limitations is that once you get to this point in the process, the lines are blurred. Limitations often become strengths. Take a look at some common strengths and limitations students identify during this final decision-making process. Worry less about whether it is a strength or limitation and more about being aware of what makes you feel your best.

STRENGTHS OR LIMITATIONS

- Makes friends quickly
- Thrives in smaller environments

- Thrives in larger environments
- Performs consistently across all academic subjects
- Performs well in areas of academic interests
- Has street smarts
- Has rural smarts
- Appreciates suburban life
- Can find something to do anywhere
- Thrives academically and socially when everything is right at their fingertips
- Doesn't mind planes, trains, and automobiles when it comes to getting places
- Needs to be able to get home within a few hours easily
- Cost is not a factor
- Cost is a factor
- Learns better on their own
- Learns better with a fully functioning resource center
- Enjoys the give-and-take of class participation
- Likes to be more anonymous in the classroom environment
- Wants to be a big fish in a small pond
- Wants to be a small fish in an ocean
- Prefers intellectual discussions during free time
- Prefers attending athletic events or participating in Greek life

The list can go on and on. But knowing where you thrive, what makes you feel fulfilled, and whom you want to be around needs to be factored into the decision. Being honest with yourself is at the core of Soundbite.

When students are having a hard time making a final decision and they reach out for help, I often first ask what their strengths and limitations are. I am always amazed at how quickly students can identify these areas at this point in the process compared to the beginning. It is a reminder that once we become self-aware, at whatever age or stage, it is a transformational moment because everything about ourselves becomes so much clearer.

But being self-aware is just one of the three traits that allows us to live by our Soundbite. Intentionality, discussed in Chapter 6, is freeing and bold when you do it. But it is not always as easy to pursue at this stage of the process. Students often feel the pressure to live up to others' expectations, or they simply are afraid to act on their intentions.

When high school seniors don't know where to enroll, I tell them to home in on just a few choices. The reality is that the student is usually seriously considering only a few colleges. As much as they feel flattered by admission to certain colleges or enticed by certain merit scholarships, they need to pare down that list to only those that are serious contenders.

Once the student has narrowed down their choices to two or three, I encourage them to be intentional and deliberate with their decision-making process:

- Visit the campus again or for the first time if possible.
- Review the communication and efforts each college has made after admission.
- Engage equally with each college being considered (online, in person, by phone, etc.).

Even after some of these exercises, some students still cannot make a decision. When fear or other factors are limiting a student's intentionality at this stage of the process, I encourage them to turn the tables. This is when I tell them to identify the strengths and limitations of the colleges they are considering.

Do they want a big rah-rah college experience with Division I sports, tailgating, and televised events?

What if the student is not a partier or not into Greek life? Does each college have a large and active alternative scene for nonpartiers?

If the student wants a tight-knit community where they know their professors well and don't feel like a number, they should be focusing on choices that provide that sort of community.

This goes for everything on their wish list: students should be considering each choice in front of them and whether each college matches up with what they want. When a student is intentional about what they want and need from their college experience, and when they measure what each college will deliver, the student gets closer to the final decision.

And that is when they can begin to embrace their story and share it with others. That last trait, storytelling, is an important last step in making a final decision. I tell students that each college they are considering gets a day to be top dog:

- Wake up, try one college on for size, fit, and feel.
- Put that college's sweatshirt on.
- Talk to your immediate family as if you are going to enroll there.
- Make a draft of an email, social media post, or conversation you plan to share with others.
- Write it out.
- Spell it out.
- Say it aloud.
- Spend your entire day, from sunrise to sunset (or even later), imagining yourself committed to attending that college.
- Lay in bed thinking about that choice.
- Does it feel right?
- Are you thinking about another college?
- Do you feel like you are missing out on something at that other college? Is that really important?

And because I believe in the Soundbite approach so much, look at the spot on your wall or next to your bed where your Soundbite is written out. Add the college's name to that Post-it, note, or poster board. Does that college truly match up with your Soundbite?

The next day do the same thing with the other college(s). Doing this exercise with all of their choices gives the student a safe moment to tell their story to those closest to them without committing until they are ready.

When you imagine sharing your story officially (in whatever way you feel comfortable), the choice should enable you to live the Soundbite you want. And if your Soundbite changes, your choice should provide the resources and environment to enable that evolution. If it does not, students often consider the transfer admissions process. But remember that if the first college is not what you expected or hoped for, it is time for a pivot.

Where you enroll in college is not the end of your Soundbite. It is only the beginning. Live it until you are ready for change.

CHAPTER 16

Soundbite Now and for the Future

As tough as the college admissions process can be, it prepares us for the rest of our lives. It allows us to examine who we are, how we present ourselves to others, and how quickly others judge us. To get the most out of this experience, we need to go into it with a plan. That plan is our Soundbite.

If the rules of Soundbite are followed, it packs quite a punch. It is concise, inspiring, and truly distinctive. Soundbite also protects our own integrity and the integrity of the process. It is built on truth, authenticity, and action rather than lies, connections, and unfulfilled promises.

Soundbite took on greater meaning after the admissions scandal of 2019 broke, when it was revealed that students were being admitted based on falsified information, including lies about athletic abilities and cheating on standardized tests. All the implicated families had one thing in common: they were financially well-off and well connected. They used their money to buy better test scores, create fake résumés, and bribe athletic coaches to support their children in the admissions process.

While this scandal revealed the deception that some families, college counselors, test prep tutors, collegiate coaches, and other university employees engage in, it also shined a light on how differently students are treated in the admissions process. Whether some admissions officers and deans of admissions looked the other way or not, it is clear that students coming from "regular" backgrounds are held to the highest standards and students coming from these far-from-regular backgrounds are not.

If we were to take a look at the Soundbites written by admissions officers for the students who were admitted under false pretenses, it would be obvious even to the casual observer that the student was not deserving of admission. And if we got those implicated students to tell us their Soundbites, their true colors would be revealed. AOs are trained to see the dupe. Frankly, any untrained eye could see the dupe.

It is shocking that admissions offices have escaped from the scandal seemingly unscathed. They are breathing a sigh of relief. But their reading and decision-making process is now filled with verification procedures, more oversight, and pressure to never accept anything but authenticity from *all* students. Authenticity in admissions matters more than ever—on the part of both admissions offices and the students involved.

I was hoping for a sense of relief after the scandal broke. Yet students coming from "regular" families and backgrounds worry even more about how they can compete with students coming from these far-from-regular families. They don't have the money, connections, and arrogance.

They don't need any of it. They just need their Soundbite. In fact, those kids from extraordinary wealth and circumstances need Soundbites more than ever as well. For the first time, they will be held to the same high standards by which every "regular" kid has been measured for decades.

The truth is that the Soundbite concept was born many years before the admissions scandal occurred. Even as an entry-level AO, I was frustrated with how quickly students were judged in the application process and how the cards were often stacked against the regular kids applying to college. At my core, I am still that regular kid from New Jersey trying to do something extraordinary.

When I became a college counselor, I needed to find a solution to deal with the speed and competition of the process. I didn't want students to be dismissed unfairly. I wanted them to see themselves in the most spectacular light. I have always believed that is half the battle.

Along the way, I realized that the college admissions process was a lot like applying to graduate school, getting jobs, and building a business. Everything has to line up perfectly (or appear to) for us to reach our goals. Regular kids and regular adults cannot rely on family money and family connections. If we get something, it is because we earned it. And while we often don't always get what we deserve, when we do, it means much more.

The best way to get something is to earn it. But that means we need to work on ourselves and our plan to achieve what we want. Soundbite keeps us focused on what matters to us the most. It helps young people and adults invest time into what they can control.

Admissions officers should not define who students are. Where we go to college shouldn't define us either. It is up to us to define who we are, but we need to do it in the most effective way for others to see what we see in ourselves.

If you know you will be judged in minutes or seconds but you have something extraordinary to do, then write it down in the last exercise of this book. Hold it close to you. Let it guide you. Live it every single day—unless, of course, it is no longer true, accurate, or fulfilling. And then pivot to your even more evolved self. Rewrite your Soundbite as needed. If the rules are followed every time, your Soundbite will open the gates to higher education and every opportunity that follows.

FINAL SOUNDBITE EXERCISE

Write your Soundbite here:

_____

_____

_____

_____

1. Is it written in the first person? ☐ Yes ☐ No

2. Is it one concise sentence (forty words or fewer)? ☐ Yes ☐ No

3. Is it written in the present tense? ☐ Yes ☐ No

4. Are nouns and verbs used instead of adjectives and adverbs?
    ☐ Yes ☐ No

5. Is it true that no one else in the world could have the same Soundbite as
    you? ☐ Yes ☐ No

If you answered yes to all five questions, you have your Soundbite. Now
live it.

Conclusion

Some things are out of our control, like the circumstances we are born into, the family we are a member of, and our race. We cannot control natural disasters, scandals, pandemics, or the past. But we can control how we live our lives and how we project ourselves to others. That's our Soundbite. Our truth.

Soundbite has the power to change our lives and those around us. No matter what we face—whether our parents are immigrants, we are immigrants, or we come from low-income households or dysfunctional homes, struggle with mental or physical disorders, or have enjoyed seemingly unremarkable yet positive upbringings—we must use this as fuel to uncover who we are, what makes us different, and how we can positively contribute to the world around us in the most breathtaking and moving way.

Inherent in the Soundbite approach, though, is a willingness to articulate, project, and live our Soundbite. This means that we cannot hope that others recognize our specialness, talents, or good deeds. We must recognize them and effectively communicate them to our educators, admissions officers, interviewers, future bosses, and mentors. While we craft our own Soundbite, these individuals have the power to open doors for us. If we don't make a positive and impactful impression on them, including through the college application, how can we expect them to open those doors for us?

Soundbite transforms the humblest student into his own best advocate. Soundbite transforms the student with so much to say into the student who chooses her words carefully in order to have the most impact. Soundbite transforms the student who is lost in someone else's shadow or can't get out of his own shadow to become the best version of himself.

It is about taking charge of your life. Moms, dads, guardians, mentors, and friends can be supportive of what we want, but it is ultimately up to us as individuals to craft our Soundbites.

Soundbites need to be short and sweet. Something we remember. Something others remember about us.

Holding onto the past limits our potential. Focusing too much on the future ignores what we could be doing now. "I was" shows a reliance on the past. "I want" does not guarantee anything in the future. "I am" is the embodiment of living in the present and taking advantage of opportunity. Our Soundbites must be anchored in our present lives.

I want all of us to be activators rather than modifiers in every environment in which we find ourselves. We shouldn't rely on common pursuits. We shouldn't rely on adjectives and adverbs when describing ourselves. We should use nouns to claim our roles and experiences and verbs to show evidence of our actions. In an era when truth matters, nouns and verbs are verifiable.

And in the end, a Soundbite that is truly unique to us and no one else will empower us to do something profound. I don't want to go through life doing and saying what others do and say. Neither do you.

I may be an ordinary girl from New Jersey with no connections. But I can do extraordinary things. In fact, I am doing that right now. So can you.

Whether you are interested in an Ivy League university, an obscure liberal arts college, or an institution with a high acceptance rate, you need to have a Soundbite. Because if you want to go to college, you have goals in mind. They may not be formed quite yet. However, your Soundbite can be formed right now.

Our past does not define us, and nor should our college. Attending a highly ranked college is no more than an achievement that soon becomes something in the past. It is what we do while in college and with the education we receive that has the most impact on ourselves and society.

Soundbite holds no prejudice. Anyone can write and live their Soundbite. If we speak our truth and live our truth, others will understand and recognize what we have to offer. We won't be misunderstood. We will see ourselves clearly and in the best possible way, and others will view us similarly.

No matter what happens in the college admissions landscape, Soundbite will always be relevant. Whether colleges eliminate standardized tests, require something else instead, or face challenging times that force them to admit more students rather than fewer, we must craft and live our own Soundbite in order to thrive in a changing world. Soundbites evolve as we evolve. Colleges will have to do the same.

Soundbites help in every stage of life. Graduate school, job interviews, business proposals, inventions, parenthood, and even retirement will challenge us in ways we never anticipated. Armed with a positive, powerful, and distinctive Soundbite, we will never lose our way. The Soundbite will help us make the right decisions to ensure our truth, our impact, and our legacy.

Helpful Exercises When You Have Trouble Coming Up with Your Soundbite

Whenever students have trouble coming up with their Soundbite or a possible academic major to list on their applications, I go back to my own memories of being a high school student. I was unsure of who I was, what I was good at, and what to do with it. That person I was in high school showed signs of distinctiveness and academic passion, whether I realized it or not, but I desperately needed the Soundbite concept back then. My goal is to make sure no student feels lost, unremarkable, or misguided along the way ever again.

One of the solutions for students struggling with their Soundbite and potential major is to take a common exercise that many college counselors, teachers, and even applications ask to help get a better sense of the student. For example, college counselors and teachers often ask students to fill out a "brag sheet" or questionnaire before they write a recommendation letter. This is supposed to help them get to know the student better, but it can easily turn into a crutch, with the student's answers getting copied into the letter of recommendation almost verbatim. I always warn students to fill these forms out thoughtfully because they could essentially be writing part of their own recommendation letter without even realizing it. One of the most popular prompts on the questionnaires asks the student to describe himself in a few words. To be more specific, sometimes the prompt explicitly says to use five adjectives.

As you know, adjectives are not my favorite way to describe anyone. I always like students to use nouns and verbs when crafting their Soundbite. The same thing goes for answering this popular prompt.

Recently, a mom indicated that her child was not comfortable providing his college counselor with nouns or verbs when he was asked to describe himself using five adjectives. I smiled, knowing that I was a strict rule follower in high school. But providing nouns instead of adjectives in a questionnaire for a letter writer is not something a student would get in trouble for. It would send a message to the college counselor that the student was different and, most of all, described himself differently too.

The mom asked me for an example. The first thing that came to me were five words I would use to describe my high school self. Here's what I came up with:

1. Speech
2. Ethics
3. White House (I know, it's two words, not one.)
4. 4′11″
5. Feminist

Here's why:

The only thing I felt like I really excelled at in high school was speech giving. I took public speaking as an elective class, but it wasn't a core class in the eyes of colleges. Yet every time I gave a speech, I shone in ways that were obvious to my teachers and classmates. Whether I was in English class, at the end-of-year tennis banquet, or making an announcement on the school's loudspeaker, I was in my element. Giving a speech was my special talent even going back to my early years as a kid. I can even remember being asked to be the emcee in fourth grade in a school-wide assembly. While I wasn't sure how public speaking could help me in college, I recognized that I could turn this into something more.

Ethics defined me, then and now. I was one of those kids who held herself to a high standard and never wanted to break any rules, lie, or get into trouble. There were moments when I was embarrassed by being such a rule follower. It didn't make me popular. But it gave me strength not to succumb to peer pressure even when everyone else around me was. It is all about how we see strengths in ourselves even when we are made fun of.

And while I didn't have a lot of experience winning elections in high school, my goal was to someday become the first female president of the United States. I know, very lofty. Very future focused. But like most high school students, I had big dreams.

What's interesting is that these words were the beginnings of my Soundbite and spoke to who I would become in college. I ended up majoring in communication. I won several public speaking competitions every year. And I even got to give the speech at my college graduation. Public speaking is still a huge part of my daily life.

Ethics continued to have a large presence in my four years of college. By senior year, I became the chair of the Judicial Board, serving as the arbiter for student disciplinary offenses on campus. It was not an easy position to be in as a student, but it was one I took great pride in doing. Of course, I ended up going to law school for a year after college, but just as most Soundbites evolve, mine did too. Yet, I still put ethics above all else, no matter what I am pursuing.

And wanting to make history as the first female president of the United States led me to initially plan to major in political science or government in college. I had dabbled in some political clubs in high school, but I was not exactly "electable" back then. I think I was the least popular kid in my grade. It didn't matter, though. I realized how easy it was to change my mind. In fact, like most college students, I didn't have to declare a major until spring semester of sophomore year. And my final major wasn't the first one I declared.

For those of you struggling with your Soundbite or knowing what major to list on your applications, start by writing five words (nouns or verbs only) about yourself that, when combined, no one else could say about themselves. Those five words not only become the foundation of your Soundbite but can also point out a possible major to list on your application.

Step 1: List your five words here:

1.
2.
3.
4.
5.

Step 2: Describe why each word is so indicative of you. Provide classes, grades, awards, activities, and experiences that showcase why these words are truly authentic to you.

1.
2.
3.
4.
5.

Step 3: Is there an obvious connection between two or three of the words? Or are they all distinct from each other?

Step 4: Are there any defining traits that influence you (e.g., background, physical characteristic, major obstacle, or family situation)? For me, I always loved my short stature. People underestimated me, and I used it to my advantage.

Step 5: Using verbs, more nouns, articles, conjunctions, and other nonadjective and nonadverbs to make a full sentence about yourself, tie together two or three of your words (or versions of your words) below to create a Soundbite. Here's a Soundbite I could have written for myself back in high school:

> Don't be fooled by my stature, as I use my voice to give speeches about politics, ethics, and breaking the "glass ceiling" for my generation of women.

List your Soundbite here:

_____

_____

_____

_____

Majors are not required, but listing one can surely help an admissions officer identify with your application and intentions. AOs know that students change their minds. But when it comes to the admissions process, a clear vision about what a student thinks they want to study in college can help substantiate their application.

By looking at your Soundbite, you can usually identify at least one area of academic interest. And remember that colleges usually have dozens of majors to choose from. So even if your academic passion is not a core class in high school, it can turn into a major in college and a career down the road.

For example, based on my words that I picked to describe myself and my high school Soundbite, I can identify several academic majors/disciplines that I was interested in as a high school student:

1. Communication
2. Prelaw
3. Government/political science

By looking at your activities, honors, classes, and grades in the classes you love, you can begin to identify possible major choices. As long as you have the evidence to back it up, you will now be able to do the Map It Out! Exercise from Chapter 6 and move on from there!

Examples of Soundbites That Worked

I am a state-winning powerlifter and a historian, uncovering the lost stories of medieval England, driven to deliver change based on the lessons from the past. (College of William & Mary)

I am a writer (with a knack for math as well), and I use my family's own struggles and triumphs in my writing to show the fragility of life and the human capacity to evolve. (Cornell University)

I am a second-generation Greek American dedicated to my family, neighborhood, and country, and being an Eagle Scout trained in emergency preparedness allows me to serve and protect the people where I come from. (Boston College)

I am a classic rock guitarist who plays with music legends on stage, and I am a budding physicist with college-level experience and research. (University of California, Berkeley)

My business skills come from growing up surrounded by my parents' small business in our home and allowed me to grow my own baking company and website into a profit-making venture and a vehicle to give back to my community. (Indiana University)

I am interested in both the theatrics of the courtroom through my role as a lead trial attorney in Mock Trial *and* the behind-the-scenes work of contracts and labor law through my legal internship. (Tufts University)

I see communication as a vehicle to solving societal issues, whether it's at the YMCA serving as a role model to our youth or when I'm posting informative videos to Instagram and YouTube on easy fixes to technology problems. (Davidson College)

I am a second-degree black belt in Kenpo Karate, which has taught me to be decisive and precise, and these skills help me in the male-dominated world of robotics. (Rensselaer Polytechnic Institute)

I see medicine through the lens of the elderly from my four years working at an assisted-living center, which gives me a deep understanding of the aging process and how it affects the human body, mind, and spirit. (Bowdoin College)

I am creative at my core, which has led me to start writing books at an early age and to spend much of my free time engaged in developing story/poetry ideas in my writing and sketching. (Dickinson College)

I pursue the intersection of statistics, business, and sports and especially the application of data analytics to influence sports organizational decisions. (Vanderbilt University)

I am a hydrogeology "rock star" and work on developing an innovative filtration system to provide access to clean potable water worldwide. (University of Pittsburgh)

I am a military child who has relocated eight times, including twice overseas, instilling an appreciation for the impact the US has on the world, while remaining calm in the face of adversity to lead my family, teammates, and peers. (United States Military Academy)

I use my voice, through music, public speaking, and moviemaking, to transform the place I live into an inclusive environment by encouraging dialogue, organizing community fundraisers, and working on a grassroots level. (Brown University)

I am a young woman of color, member of a national cheer championship team, and UCA All-American cheerleader living in a racially charged town in the Deep South and advocating for diversity and inclusion. (Northeastern University)

I strategize solutions on my second-place world championship robotics team and as a writer creating "wins" for humanity on race, gender, and equality. (University of Texas, Austin)

I am a Filipino-Russian American who has moved many times, which allows me to adapt in domestic and foreign environments, where I represent diversity of all kinds. (Rice University)

I create safer trails in the wilderness for mountain bikers like myself by envisioning and implementing solutions and training others to improve water-eroded trails using only hand tools and ingenuity. (University of California, Santa Barbara)

I am a youth worship leader and award-winning orator making an impact and changing the trajectory of any group I am a part of with earned recognition as student body prefect, community servant, and Congressional Award winner. (Georgetown University)

I am a classicist with a special affinity for constitutional law as evidenced by my cross-country trip to observe the Supreme Court of the United States in action. (Yale University)

I am a two-sport athlete and the sole male among ten female siblings and cousins in the fifth generation of a farming family, who, through grassroots campaigning for local candidates, recognizes the strength and impact of the female political voice. (Wesleyan University)

I am a person of color, born of a mixed-raced mother and African American father, inspired by global relations, different cultures, and languages around the world, using dance and yoga as a way of uniting people of various nationalities. (University of Miami)

I am a nationally winning video game designer using my computer programming skills and artistic expression to create the most technologically advanced video games for my generation. (Carnegie Mellon University)

Extra Soundbites and Essay Topics

I often get asked by families if the student's main essay should be about something in their Soundbite. I have two different answers to this question depending on the student's Soundbite.

For the student whose Soundbite is less academic or less extracurricular in focus *or* has other pieces to it, it's possible for the student to pick one aspect out of their Soundbite and write their main essay about it, as long as they are not writing about academics or extracurricular involvement. Remember that the Soundbite never is written anywhere in the application by the student, so it is perfectly acceptable to write a main essay about something in the Soundbite.

If the student's Soundbite is heavily focused on an academic interest or extracurricular pursuit, their main essay should not be about one of these topics. In fact, they should save academic interests and extracurricular activities for supplemental essays, not the main essay. However, their main essay can complement the Soundbite.

For guidance, take a look at the examples below of some of my Application Nation students' Soundbites and main essay topics. Sometimes their main essays were directly related to something in their Soundbite, and other times their main essay simply or gently complemented their Soundbite.

STUDENTS WHO DIRECTLY REFERENCED THEIR SOUNDBITES IN THEIR MAIN ESSAY

STUDENT #1

Soundbite: I am that person who is always there for a friend, family member, or classmate who is struggling in everyday life or during larger moments in their lives, and this leads me to my passion for forensic nursing, which values solutions, healing, and justice for victims.

Essay Topic: I met one of my best friends in the first grade through soccer, and he struggles with anxiety. From fourth grade on, I was placed in classes with him because I was one of his closest friends, and he focused better when he knew people. I went to his counseling sessions because he opened up better when I was there. I learned from this to always help others and do what you can to make others feel like they have a place in this world and know that they matter.

STUDENT #2

Soundbite: I capture sunrises on film and in my mind, giving me clarity in math and science and the ability to see how the study of the brain impacts nature, our outlook, and the world around us.

Essay Topic: There's one thing that I can consistently rely on to remind me how beautifully complicated, amazing, and simple life can be every day: the sunrise. This is why I became a sunrise chaser, both literally and metaphorically.

STUDENT #3

Soundbite: Playing football is all about the detail I see, which also allows me to appreciate the impact and subtlety of my trips to ten national parks, historic architecture, and mathematical and scientific processes in ways others do not see.

Essay Topic: My family's RV is our "spaceship," allowing us to travel to a whole new world every time we visit a national park.

STUDENT #4

Soundbite: I am the son of a Marine Corps veteran who gave me an extra layer of resilience, and I carry this with me years after his death, as nothing gets in the way of me savoring opportunities on the field with my soccer teammates and saving lives as an EMT.

Essay Topic: My dad's Marine Corps phrase "Pain is weakness leaving the body" never made sense to me until he got sick. But I now use this philosophy every single day to overcome challenges and become the strongest person I can be.

STUDENT #5

Soundbite: I am a second-generation Cuban American and use my passion for politics, global current affairs, history, and public speaking to raise awareness in others through political activism and coaching younger Latino high school students in speech and debate skills.

Essay Topic: My sense of identity and purpose have been shaped by being a second-generation Cuban American, personal experiences with discrimination, and family history.

STUDENT #6

Soundbite: I am a first-generation Thai American using my culture's gracious hospitality to lead as the president of my school's business magnet program, and growing up in a tourist destination allows me to see commerce through the eyes of the consumer.

Essay Topic: I am most influenced by my culture as a Thai American and the Thai tradition of hospitality, which serves as the backbone of how I treat people—friends and strangers alike.

STUDENT #7

Soundbite: Having heart surgery may have stopped my baseball career, but it hasn't stopped me from using my artistic and entrepreneurial skills to deliver art bags to kids during quarantine and executing a virtual baseball tournament to raise money for charity.

Essay Topic: After having two major surgeries in the span of six months, I realized the silver lining of life and how I lead with my heart more than ever.

STUDENT #8

Soundbite: I represent duality as an artist and a quantitative thinker and as an American and a Japanese American, driven to use my culture, language, and history to create artistically and educationally driven computer games for children.

Essay Topic: Growing up in my homogenous community, I was often stereotyped as just another Asian student. But the moment I saw the Buddha statues in Japan and how each one was carefully constructed in its own way, I realized the value my culture places on individuality.

STUDENT #9

Soundbite: I am dedicated to the intersection of science and humanity, as I know from being born with birth-related hemiplegia the impact one person can have on another, which leads me to do things some believed I could never do.

Essay Topic: I was the third triplet born after what my mom says were the longest fifteen minutes of her life; my resulting left side hemiplegia defined the early years of my life, and I am the poster child for early intervention and the importance of family and grit.

EXAMPLES OF MAIN ESSAYS THAT DON'T REPEAT BUT GENTLY COMPLEMENT THE SOUNDBITE

STUDENT #10

Soundbite: My passion for playing football has shifted to a love of coaching, leading, and serving not only my varsity football team, of which I am the captain, but also my fellow neighbor.

Essay Topic: When my dad left our family, I lost my best friend. And I lost my way for a while. But seeing how much my mom and younger siblings needed me made me realize I was right where I belonged.

STUDENT #11

Soundbite: I view history like a symphony with different musicians, intentions, and ideas coming together as one, but at the core of understanding historical moments is observing the individuals who lead, follow, thrive, and suffer to ensure harmony in the future.

Essay Topic: Reflecting on interactions with my aunt, who has multiple sclerosis, provides me with perspective and empathy, which helps me appreciate and respect people for who they are. During her most recent extended stay with our family, my aunt surprised me with even more life lessons and reminded me that I have much to learn.

STUDENT #12

Soundbite: I build connections between the humanities and the sciences as a research assistant to a *NYT* best-selling author, a leader of a National Science Foundation project, and as a facilitator teaching young kids about philosophy and science.

Essay Topic: Rural white southern family meets urban brown immigrant family . . . and I'm in the middle of it, which has brought shocking heartbreak but mostly a deep appreciation for the difficulty and transcendence of navigating differences.

STUDENT #13

Soundbite: My family has always taught me to "pass the ball," share the spotlight, and do the right thing—and while this may seem fundamental, I live by these actions and let others see the power of kindness.

Essay Topic: "Freshman backpack" took on a whole new meaning for me when interviewing for Peer Leaders as a freshman. In the stress of staying focused on making a good first impression, as well as making good on a promise to myself to take new chances, I somehow managed to keep my backpack on my back through the entire interview. I realize now that it served as an authentic moment representing who I am and who I strive to be.

STUDENT #14

Soundbite: My voice is heard through action as the president of the Community Service League and through my state-recognized music as a trumpeter.

Essay Topic: I live in Texas, yet I am not your typical Texan. My Mexican family has worked hard to stay in this land and has taught me that it's not where you live; it's what you do.

STUDENT #15

Soundbite: I use my theater background, public-speaking skills, and on-air TV personality to make people feel comfortable, laugh, and enjoy their everyday lives, and there is no better way to do this than in the field of hospitality.

Essay Topic: Sometimes, when everything goes wrong, it goes right, especially when a snowstorm hits and you and your dad have to drive almost one thousand miles and over twenty hours, during which you learn a lot about your dad and yourself.

STUDENT #16

Soundbite: I am a social justice advocate making access to education, health care, and the arts a reality for everyone through my music, writing, and podcast to connect with others, highlight our similarities, and bring awareness of our differences.

Essay Topic: My family is originally from North Korea, and the Hanbok my grandmother gave me is an ever-present reminder of the history of my family and the actions taken by my ancestors to fight for justice in an age of oppression.

STUDENT #17

Soundbite: I am a "viewfinder" with my camera and perspective, seeing beyond race, theories of science, classical and Japanese cultures and languages, and human behavior—because if others observe me keeping an open mind, they will too.

Essay Topic: My Brazilian grandfather came to pick me up from my first day of school, but my teacher wouldn't let me leave with him as she didn't believe he was my grandfather due to how white I looked and how foreign he looked. That moment was the first time I realized how different we looked to others, yet how similar we are in reality.

ACKNOWLEDGMENTS

I t is only fitting that my last words written on Soundbite are those of deep self-awareness, intentionality, and storytelling. I am on the cusp of handing in a full edited manuscript to my editors and publisher. I never thought I could write a one-page essay my first year of college, let alone a book about to be published, about college no less. And for that I am truly grateful for where my Soundbite began to emerge, Hamilton College.

I want to thank the Hamilton College admissions officer who read my application and saw something in me that I didn't see in myself. I don't know who you are, but you gave my story and my Soundbite room to grow.

Professor Bahlke was my favorite professor at Hamilton. I took more classes from him than any other. He taught me that it is never how loud your voice is; it is how effective it is. I will never forget the English papers I wrote for him, especially the one about Sylvia Plath, because that is when I realized I could write. He was a legend at Hamilton, and I pinch myself every day that I had a professor like him.

My brother, Louis, is the only sibling I have. He came home from his first year of college and announced he wanted to be a dean of admissions after the most amazing time he had as a college tour guide. Even then, he shared generously whether he benefited or not. While he never became a dean of admissions, he gave me the dream to become one myself. Since then, he is my most trusted confidant, serving not only as my big brother but as my attorney through every step of building my business and becoming a published author. Thank you, Louis, for always looking over my contracts and, most of all, for looking out for me.

I want to make sure that my mom knows how much I was impacted by her immigrant story. The struggles she faced gave me empathy for the many struggles my students face growing up. The immigrant story never grows old for me (or any admissions officer), and for that I am grateful to you, Mom. I highlight many immigrants and first-generation Americans in the book because of you. I have always loved your story and have loved every single immigrant story I have ever heard—because of you.

My dad schlepped me all over the Northeast in the summer of 1992, making sure I saw every college I wanted to see. I couldn't get enough of it. I loved every second of our time together that summer, Dad. I found meaning and purpose in every college we visited. You have instilled in me a love for education that fuels me and my message every day. Education is contagious, and I got my love for it from you. It is my calling, and I hope to spread it for as long as I can. Just like you have done for me.

Sarah Massari is my dearest friend and colleague. She was by my side when I had my first national TV interview and when I found out that I got a book deal. She works longer hours than anyone. I love you like a sister, Sarah. We make a great team.

I am thankful for Lauren Miller, who keeps my brand on point every single day. No matter how many curveballs get thrown her way, she manages to always articulate my truth and my message in a way that is pure and authentic, just like the Soundbite concept encourages all of us to do.

Ali Parmelee is the genius behind my websites and programs. She guided me through some of the biggest decisions I made for my business in those early years. I cannot thank you enough for your brilliance, Ali.

To the many students I encountered as an admissions officer and dean of admissions, thank you for inspiring me. Your accomplishments kept me humble and wanting more for myself.

The students at the Baldwin School gave me purpose when I needed it most. I was a washed-up dean of admissions and stay-at-home mom when I was hired to be the director of college counseling. But it was your extraordinary stories that gave me the idea of Soundbite.

For the many private clients and Application Nation students who grace the pages of this book, thank you for putting your trust in me and for believing in the Soundbite concept. Your authenticity carries me during my longest days.

Chris Park, thank you for reaching out to me. I didn't even know what a literary agent was when I started writing the proposal for this book. But you have proven every day why I needed you. I never would have gotten a book deal if it weren't for you. Thank you for making this once impossible dream a reality for me.

Dan Ambrosio, my patient and kind editor at Hachette Book Group, thank you for believing in me and *Soundbite*. The moment I met you, I could have sworn I knew you. That first meeting made me feel like I was hanging out with an old friend. I hope our friendship lasts a lifetime.

And Alison Dalafave, you are such an integral part of this book. Dan and Hachette are lucky to have you. Your edits gave me something to chew on. I would immediately wonder how I was going to incorporate them into the book. But once I did, it was like magic jumping off the page.

My three children, Sophie, Max, and Dotsie Bea, are the ultimate magic, though. They put up with my long hours of work as if it's a badge of honor. If anyone mom-shames me for working, Sophie is the first to defend me. I never have to hope that she is watching what I am doing. I know she is watching and wants to be a powerful voice in the world around her. Max is my creative. He throws himself into a world that he creates from scratch and believes wholeheartedly in it. He reminds me to always create and believe in the impossible. And Dotsie Bea is small and mighty. I hope she never stops being either. I promise, I won't.

Finally, I owe the biggest gratitude to Justin, my one and only love. He gave me life and support from the moment we locked eyes on each other on the steps of a college party. That night in the winter of 1994, he carried me up a snowy hill so that I wouldn't slip in my cowgirl boots. From that day on, he never let me slip. He taught me how to love and how to write. He sat next to me, editing my papers, teaching me grammar, and pointing out the powerful literary tools at my fingertips. For the past twenty-seven years, he has believed in my dreams. He tells our kids every single day that their mom is a superstar. But he is the ultimate star, allowing others to shine. I am no longer just America's College Counselor.

I am America's College Counselor and the author of *Soundbite* because of you, Justin.